AF423703

From
Adam
To
Eve

From
Adam
To
Eve

God's Pathway to a Successful Marriage

Married Men Only

Wale Joseph

The **First** and **Only** Book That Tells You
What… and **How**…

Publisher

Broad Range Ventures
Lagos, Nigeria.
familypivot@gmail.com
+234 1 802 101 6239 (SMS Only)

Disclaimer

Print Format: ISBN - 13: 978 - 9 - 78941 - 715 - 5

eBook Format: ISBN - 13: 978 - 9 - 78941 - 716 - 2

To all professionals who are working tirelessly to make sure that relationships are healthy and romantically intimate.

Acknowledgement

Kindly note that personal editing was done using MS Word:
https://products.office.com/en-us/word

Figures 1A, 1B, 2 and 3 were made with the use Pivot Animator software from:
http://pivot-stickfigure-animator.en.softonic.com/

The commercial versions of these super-efficient tools are available at their respective websites.

The author is using this opportunity, to show appreciation to other individuals and organizations who have contributed to the process of writing, publishing and selling of this book.

Members of the author's family are hereby acknowledged for their support and understanding. Life truly, is full of turbulence… up steps in small sizes, and down steps in giant sizes. However, every little success made is able to overshadow multiple forms of giant failures. To a great extent, these seemingly micro successes are able to compensate for all losses… to confirm the wonderfulness of God.

Finally, all glory is to God for granting His wisdom (to write) and guidance (to convert the volume to a Christian literature).

Contents

Introduction

"Happy is the man that findeth wisdom…"

Proverbs 3:13 (KJV)

Specifically, this eBook is meant for married men. Women, if married, are also welcomed. Unmarried individuals must be at least twenty-eight years old to access the contents of this book. *If you are not married, kindly pass the book on to whoever is. You'll gain more by so doing.* All persons not eligible but by chance, got a copy of this book are hereby implored in the name of our Lord Jesus Christ, not to read beyond this point.

Everyone is excited about the high rate at which marriages are formed. Yet, *baffling* is the rate at which the same bliss crashes into regret while statistical figures continue to be staggering. Somehow, this is an unfortunate cycle with no end in sight. In the meantime, technological products aren't providing solutions at the speed of light, as expected. The population of experts on marital issues has become astronomical and far-reaching philosophies have been churned out. Yet, marriages continue to break up and emotions… shredded into devastation. Religious leaders are ever baffled despite regular and seemingly adequate effort.

In an attempt to achieve marital success, watch out for the man, he is ever strong-minded. Small wonder he is annoyed when divorce becomes inevitable. In his thinking, **"Women are ever impossible."** In the same way… the woman, as she pushes through divine duties in Proverbs 31 verses 10 to 30, becomes physically and mentally exhausted, with devastation written all over her. In her thinking, **"What's the essence of this misery called marriage?"** To reverse this awful situation, what should be noteworthy is a marital idea that is scantily discussed by marital experts and often ignored by men. Cautiously, most religious leaders will stay reserved; evidently, it is difficult to draw the line when teaching this necessary notion. Meanwhile, it is a notion with enormous scientific research facts supporting its usefulness. Since marriage counselors and other experts wouldn't dare, kindly let's say that it is embedded in Paul's divine and logical insight that says…

> "…it is better to marry than to burn."
>
> 1st Corinthians 7:9 KJV

Benefits obtainable from ideal sexual exercise include crucial psychological relief, which will **recurrently generate mental vitality for women, as it is in men.** *Closely, emotional vigor will produce m*assive ability to **rekindle a glowing splint of love**, and matchless power to **create optimal marital excitement** as often as required. Therefore, to put it briefly, underlying characteristics to this marital concept will underscore the following as marital facts:

…The woman is the key to unlock marital success
The ability to ensure marital success is divinely installed in the woman.

…The man should lead by asking the woman to lead
A man may start the option that could lead to marital success; he does not have sufficient capacity with which to guarantee marital success.

…Orgasm: the divine remedy for stress
For adults, an absolutely free and divinely made remedy for stress, including that from marriage, is orgasms (and not sex). Sex is only one popular route to orgasm. Unbelievably, this knowledge is scantily shared among married individuals.

…Feminine sexual preference
To achieve orgasm, the approach preferred by a woman must be properly considered; often, the man believes he's always right.

…The woman: an amazing powerhouse
When she is recurrently made free of mental stress, the man will ever be in amazement of what a woman can accomplish, at any time and… effortlessly.

The third factor above is dominant but this is what will complicate the man's situation. This is one of the reasons for which the idea has been studied from several angles. However, a startling perspective to the concept is that an average woman would rather keep silent despite an almost unbearable concern when her experience isn't recurrent. Meanwhile, the man is ignorant of a feminine fascination that's in no way lesser than the masculine craves. Regularly worsening the situation is the fact that, a man is not sure of what to do or how…. Then, he'd turn himself into a heavy-duty machine; he's using an age-old approach that has remained a failure.

So, long before now, men had concluded that there's a wide gap between them and the members of the opposite sex in terms of sexuality and sexual response in particular. Therefore, the view of most men is that women's sexual response isn't just considerable but sometimes pondered as excessive. It may then not be out of place to associate women's sexual passivity with several reasons which might include overt intimidation from men; possibly, this is an action that's being used to shield shortfall in masculine sexuality. Meanwhile, both concealed and open attempt intended to bridge this gully have had the contribution of specialists from different fields of training, each one churning out several concepts.

Then, it shouldn't be a surprise to find out that ancient medicine had been on the race for several centuries. The quest gave an upper hand to women; it focused on men as the gender that needed to *improve*. From as far back as 1889, modern medicine joined the search effort… with a giant stride. Then, Serge Voronoff, a Surgeon, injected himself under the skin with extracts from ground-up testicles of a dog and a guinea pig. Instantly following this action were several hundreds of medical transplantation experiments, each involving grafting of testicles from younger to older animals. In his conclusion, Voronoff specified that the transplantations caused older animals to regain the vigor of younger ones in their sexual potency. Voronoff issued this result in his book titled, "Rejuvenation by Grafting," (1925). Further within the publication, he disclosed that human sex drive may be improved via this means.

Voronoff's disclosure was applauded by world's leading Surgeons at the International Congress of Surgeons in London. Then, it was a giant breakthrough, "…an end to sexual anxiety that was secretly plaguing men in every cranny of human existence," they must have thought. Therefore, by early 1930s, thousands of men around the world had received this rejuvenation technique; …wealthy men handsomely paid to access the medical procedure. A medical process that comprises the implantation of a thin slice of testicles sheared from chimpanzees and baboons, into the human scrotum!

However, many of the patients who received the surgery and praised Voronoff merely had euphoria that resulted solely from placebo effect. Subsequently, results from further research eventually exposed the inaccuracy in Voronoff's work. Since then, over one hundred and twenty-three years, men continued to search and improve on findings meant to correct this inadequacy in masculine sexual response. For this reason, colossal research effort has produced different varieties of products that could be directly ingested by men or applied by men on women, to pep up masculine sexuality. The technique or the product notwithstanding, what is clear is that the man must have a better sexual response. He should be able to cope with… and be able to give considerable sexual satisfaction to the woman and by implication, his marriage. As at today, it's easily visible that the number of people within research walls and the rate at which they work is ever on the rise. Keenly, they're pursuing sexual satisfaction for romantic relationships; this is an indication that the pursuit is yet to be over.

It is observable that professional research societies are persistently interested in devising better means by which an average man could provide sexual satisfaction for his partner, and this is a welcome idea. In the meantime, it is unfortunate that many of the products presently available are planned to augment men's sexual *performance* rather than *response*. Erroneously, this line of thought must have been based on the presumption that masculine sexuality is inadequate. If we could explore social, cultural and religious views to this issue, then it would easily be perceived that men, on the whole, would merely need to understand what to do in order to sexually satisfy women. There'd only be the need for the man to discern femininity just a little better, if sexual activities are to be carried out without the use of performance enhancement products and without the need to spend money baselessly. He'd need more awareness, if he wouldn't abdicate his sexual obligation to implements that are frequently rejected by women, using a delicate expression of an unflinching preference for the masculine ***tool***.

Up to now, there's an outlook that most people including research bodies are yet to fully admit. This is the fact that feminine sexual discontent is the most potent of *missiles*, loitering nearby every marriage. Eventually, a twist in events could crash a marriage into oblivion soon after the woman conceives how to *end* the misery via self-help. Evidently, the woman – frankly - is not asking for a heavy-duty task for the man to match up to and possibly, surpass her sexual response and desire. However, this is where a definite but untapped understanding is placed by nature. This book will try as far as possible, to expose this known yet idling knowledge; it's an absolute fact every man could use, to create sexual satisfaction in his home. Using the method, a man could effortlessly and repeatedly make his spouse attain between ten and as far as fourteen orgasms in multiple successions, before his first orgasm. Besides, this is a unique fit that an average man would bring about without an iota of exhaustion. It is a fit anyone will carry out, devoid of products meant to boost sexuality… in whichever form.

Thus, it is necessary to congratulate whoever obtained a copy of this book, ***"From Adam to Eve, God's Pathway to a Successful Marriage."*** Without a doubt, the book will illustrate exactly how a man could improve on his sexuality far beyond his mostly reserved sensual fantasy. From the man meanwhile, the only requirement is for him to understand simple, easy-to-follow steps; the use of a special product or skill is not required. If no additional capability is required, and women are repeatedly taken to the peak of sexual excitement using the mostly desired *biological* tool, easily then, they'll be pulled out of sexual passivity. Ultimately, an improved feminine input will result in mutual sexual joy for the couple. Therefore, according to the Society for the Scientific Study of Sexuality (SSSS), "…More couples will tend to be happier." Visibly then, fewer marriages will – midway - *smash against the rock.*

As a result, it is necessary to urge every man to study the method outlined in this book. Even in the first attempt, it would be observed that the technique is not intricate and categorically, the woman would observe and most likely, commend the change. The impression that a man could make a woman attain up to fourteen orgasms in a series, before he would climax the first one, sounds too flawless to be true. Recorded in this book is a process that could be practiced by any couple, regardless of social, cultural and religious background. It's an idea that's independent of age, or the anxiety within a marriage. Additionally, the issue about body or genital dimensions will become irrelevant and absolutely, couples would be willing to recommend this book.

Meanwhile, it is necessary here to quickly, say that the expressions used in, and the arrangement of this book is definitely not perfect. *The author isn't a native speaker of the English language and unfortunately, lacks training on any literary-related profession. So, keen interest, broad attention and tolerance would be vital for anyone to extract the idea herein described. However, as anyone reads through, there's a guarantee that the idea would emerge. Along with the author, simply turn the pages…*

To start with, it is necessary to know that the woman is naturally endowed to be diligent, ingenious and of high integrity, Proverbs 31 verses 10 to 30. Deliberately, she was made by God to perform a crucial role. However, as enormous as this responsibility is, the woman will ask for nothing in return except five basic concepts. The first two will be found in a regularly avoided Bible verse…

> "Give her of the fruit of her hands; and let her own works praise her in the gates,"
>
> Proverbs 31:31 (KJV)

Here, the Bible is revealing two golden rules for marital success! There are five of these crucial guidelines, these two are the basis of feminine skepticism before, while dating and through marriage. For obvious reasons, four of these guidelines would be discussed very briefly. This brevity will provide ample room for the fifth rule to be woven into the contents of this book. The fifth being the rule that'll insistently regenerate mental vitality, would keep the woman working tirelessly for compliments obtainable from any other rule, all through her marriage. Fairly devoid of difficulty, whoever has read the first book titled, "The Manly Man, How to Fill Your Relationship with Optimal Excitement," would have dug up this fifth golden rule. It is the nub of infidelity in most marriages and therefore, the reason for which practicable scheme must be uncovered. Certainly, mere observations will prove that the first four rules are the basis of most of other marriage guidebooks. However, it is worthy to note that not one of these five golden rules must be detached, as they are equally significant. Covertly, every man that goes into marriage has marital success as his aim, making the five rules inevitable masculine inputs. They'll make marriages last until the very last second of couples' existence and… effortlessly.

While craving necessary consideration, every married man is here invited on to further pages; with much tolerance, explore burrows dug on each sheet, to help string out the fifth golden rule.

Chapter 1

Masculine Trend

"Hope deferred maketh the heart sick…"

Proverbs 13:12 (KJV)

Every adult is familiar with the fact that sex, as part of marital relationships, gives the highest physical pleasure known. Undeniably, a deeper insight will also reveal that sex and orgasm in particular, are the toughest of affection mortars. In reality, they are the most effective of couple's bond that simultaneously and efficiently rekindles stress-free and delightful marriages. This is the foremost reason among many others, for which respectable individuals and organizations are part of the exploration to improve masculine sexuality and sexual response; to care for our marriages and hence the family, the basic social unit of every society.

Of course, the search to improve on masculine sexuality and sexual response is the objective of this book. With a better sexual response, a man would effortlessly co-opt his able partner, to protect his marriage and hence his family. Therefore, naturally embedded in this goal is how an average man would successfully bring his wife out of sexual passivity, to make her benefit from sex and orgasms… in the best way possible. In this fashion, she'd experience the peak of physical pleasure. Gradually also, this pleasure would build up, to make her a happy, helpful wife and partner. Surely then, feminine orgasms would be needed in the desired manner and using the preferred method. Then, the necessary psychological relief would be provided so the woman could happily exhibit and utilize her God given capability as an appropriate help for the man… Genesis 2:18. From then on, and without reservation, she'd unveil a divine *desire* for her husband. Genesis 3:16.

Another vital benefit that might also be gained from this book is a decline in masculine sexual infidelity. Multiple orgasms offer the smartest approach that could pull any woman out of sexual passivity, to exhibit overt feminine sexual activity and a copious sexual input. An increase in feminine **sexual activity** will constitute much enough stimuli for the man; definitely, this would build a surge in **sexual excitement** for him. Visibly, this is where a woman – often inadvertently - would be able to generate the kind of sexual pleasure that virtually every man hunts for in extramarital affairs. This is the point where the man will perceive and positively respond to intense sexual delight that'll ooze from his wife. Therefore, it is the point at which masculine sexual infidelity could subside, to make the home what he… the man, planned it to be.

Definitely, no one is a superhuman in any way. Also, the use of any product – dietary, medicinal or physical tool purposely to boost sexual act - will not be pondered. Yet, we will get to share the truth that an average man is not sexually deprived. A man is designed to balance, or even surpass and satiate his spouse sexually regardless of how appalling in sexual dexterity he is. Without getting tired, he could make his woman reach multiple orgasms up to…; a perfect clue that he isn't sexually disadvantaged! Then, we may reach a pact at the end that the biological composition of women is so complete that they are able to match men in every way, and that includes sex.

The woman is the one designed to complement the man; reasoning the other way round is erroneous. Over several centuries, this is the belief that's secretly ruined countless number of marriages the world over. At this point, it is necessary to say here that the method described in this book takes certain vital issues for granted. These issues include the following:

> … **That** sex partners are married to one another.
> … **The** method presumes the absence of Sexually Transmitted Diseases (STDs) in both partners and that they are aware of and ready to take further responsibility for casual sexual activities, due to absolute exposure to STDs including HIV, where multiple partners exist.

... Either partner is totally liable over incidences of unwanted or uninvited pregnancy.

... Using strong expressions, this writer discourages the use of drugs by either partner, to boost sexual activity. If needed however, a medical doctor is the only person competent enough, to handle sexuality matters including whatever method that could be used for its enhancement.

... The method described in this book, is based innocently on the personal experience and logic of over twenty years by the author, without reference to any medical opinion.

Therefore, what would be unveiled is an honest idea that'll fantastically improve sexual excitement and desire in the woman and ultimately, her love for her man. It's an idea that'll particularly boost a man's sexual confidence, and stupendously enlarge his ego and personal joy. This is because in simple terms, it's a method requiring only the following:

... One hundred percent of self: that is, just the way the man is and whatever body or penile size.

... Zero products to boost sexuality: the intake of products, in whichever form, to boost sexuality is absolutely pointless. Seeking ways to elongate men's sexual response is likewise needless. The only exception is where the man's action must be based on medical advice.

... Zero to ordinary body exercises: there's no need for special physical exercises, except what is normal for an individual and probably already in the daily routine.

The method described in this small book will prove that all other approaches hitherto used to boost sexuality, are entirely unnecessary, for an excellent masculine sexual *performance* to occur. Particularly, it'll show that it's not necessary to lengthen sexual period in an attempt to make a woman attain orgasm. It's a method that guarantees not just an orgasm but a rapid array of multiple orgasms. Besides, it'll assist either partner to comprehend the enormous capability that's inherent in the average man. By this method, the woman would be tugged pleasingly close to her man; she'd admire him more passionately. Clearly, this is because of a huge pleasant surprise about the man that will be uncovered. The associated gladness will not only be evident in the woman but will mutually radiate back and forth, between either partner. Added to marital joy, the technique will bring down the cost previously incurred when sexuality enhancement products were being purchased. It'll also moderate, if not totally cut off, the side effects from certain varieties of products meant to boost sexuality.

By a subjective observation, one would understand that a greater proportion of women than men, do not despise a humble beginning in all aspects of human endeavor. It is agreeable that women have the ability to perform when circumstances are encouraging, but they tend to be eager more than men, to ameliorate and change situations right when life incidents mandate so. Hence, at a low social-financial level, they persevere more than men. Vis-à-vis marital affairs, the situation would be found to be the same. So, a greater percentage of women than men would go into a marriage with the belief that situations would in the end, be favorable or they could… and would logically make alterations. Agonizingly, unnecessary perseverance will combine with the awareness that women do not get a new romantic relationship going as easily as men do, when it becomes inevitable to change spouse for whatever reason.

Although, a split up with a partner might frequently be unavoidable in the young due to youthful exuberance, however, feminine counterparts would still be observable to be reserved in this regard. So, the woman is more willing to persevere and revamp her ailing romantic relationship as regularly as required. In the same way, this occurrence is often found to take place in a bedroom situation, where it would be glaringly observable in the woman's attitude, though made as covertly as possible. For instance, when the man is sure that he's had a poor sexual *display*, most likely, she'd provide women's standard response, "I'm okay…" with a subtle shrug, after a query. In a flimsy attempt to further persuade the man, she might say that, "An orgasm during sex is not mandatory for women.…" This is a widespread reaction from women and it is so prevalent irrespective of culture or development.

From a simple mental analysis, she isn't okay! A good proportion of women are not satisfied. By using this response, the woman is trying to *kill **several** birds with one stone*. Accordingly, issues she's trying to tackle might include the following:

… Not to tarnish her man's ego

After a visible expression of orgasmic pleasure by the
man and sexual fulfillment a little after, then, she's the one
who could tell that the gratification was biased. Nonetheless,
her thinking is that she could debilitate the man's self-esteem
by using obvious verbal words to describe his unacceptable
sexual *performance*.

… To prevent unwanted reactions

The feminine philosophy here is that the man's weakened ego
would eventually lead up to chains of unwanted reactions
from him. Therefore, she's got to nib an imminent mess as
early as possible.

… To avoid negative ideas about her sexuality

Here she's trying to suppress the situation where the man
could mention, or even consider any adverse view about her
sexuality; an evaluation she'd presumed the man would get
wrong. Thus, she'd try to keep all vulgarisms out of the man's
thought and of course, out of her relationship.

Meanwhile, tension would keep mounting for the woman as
she goes through several weeks of sexual activities and yet deprived
of an orgasm. Most likely afterwards, she'll attempt self-help the
moment she reflects that endurance and waiting are apparently endless. To rectify this needless wait, the solution devised by some wom-
en in modern times, might include secretly making use of sex toys. At
times, this action is when their partner is away. In some way, *the fact is
that majority of women are never inspired by the sight of these implements*; but
sometimes, humans have to make do with what they see. Certainly,
the utmost desire of an average woman is to share sexual intimacy
with her spouse and not a mechanical device… not even when such
an improvisation is lifelike! Every man would need to watch out for
that covert sigh, to understand that women have adamant and inex-
plicable love for nature.

During an intercourse, another common trend is where the
man would deliberately and sometimes painstakingly deploy every
effort, to ensure an orgasm for his spouse. Even with an orgasm at
every other intercourse, the man would have only achieved very little
in terms of sexual satisfaction for the woman. This occurrence might
be difficult to believe, but it is true for most women. Most men do
not realize the mess because an average woman would forever keep

mute about feminine sexuality; it's up to whoever… to discover. In the meantime, due to the lack of orgasmic pleasure, the woman would have to look for ways to cope with mental stress building up within.

> "Hope deferred maketh the heart sick: but when the desire cometh, it is a tree of life."
>
> Proverbs 13:12 (KJV)

It is often said that the man is more easily and quickly aroused than the woman. This is erroneous as either sex partner is motivated from the same perspectives which are frequently divided into three: initial, actual and post sexual act. Each of these parts could be alienated further into at least, three respective steps. In particular, the first part could be expanded into: personal craving, amorous scenery and decisive inducement steps. Regardless of the total number of steps obtainable, it is clear that women possess and exploit the capability to savor each step at a stunningly gradual and desirable pace. However, once sexual interest has been identified, thereafter, most men would hastily jump into *action* and in no time, are through long before their partner is half way up… Obviously in this way, the woman would be left half way into excitement. Anyhow, she will have to demonstrate the comportment that'll not discourage the man. More accurately, she wouldn't want to condemn her man's poor sexual response, so as not to hurt the relationship she's built. This has been discussed fully, in the fourth chapter of the leading book titled, "The Manly Man – How to Fill Your Relationship with Optimal Excitement." So, the issue is easily identifiable and it's one for which the man should be blamed. As a result, an observable situation is that…:

> *… Most married women will go through several weeks of sexual activities at a desired frequency, and often devoid of an orgasm. A situation that's not ideal by any standard: medical, social… even religious.*

Chapter 2

Distractions

"So ought men to love their wives as their own bodies…. For no man ever yet hated his own flesh…"

Ephesians 5:28 & 29 (KJV)

For a woman to express her sexuality before her spouse as she desires shouldn't be a perturbing occurrence. It's got nothing to do with an unwanted tendency to marital dishonesty. As a result of this and whatever other reason one might add, plus being sensitive to and appreciative of one's spouse's sexuality, some men have taken strides to brighten their sexual situation. Men, definitely not all, have tried to pep up their sexuality…. This might though be commendable, but several of the available tools are erroneously directed at sexual *performance* rather than *response*. Reasonably, a great number of men made use of means that vary from food to physical exercise and as far as drugs. It's delightful that some of these methods do provide positive results; they are commonly obtained via the advice of aptly qualified personnel. However, here in this book, **is a sexual method that does not require the use of material products in whatever form,** to boost men's sexual response.

Despite the absence of material products to enhance sexual response, **there's a guarantee that an average man would be able to give his spouse a minimum of ten multiple orgasms, in a quick succession, during a single sexual session.** This will also be done without the least of tiredness, particularly for the man. The method is neither laborious nor boring in any way and could be repeated as regularly as the frequency of sexual contact between couples.

For now, rather than a consideration for a boost in sexual performance, it would be pertinent to reflect on what may cause distractions, which would in turn cause a reduced or an outright diversion of concentration and hence, how to avoid them. It might be better to categorize what may cause such distractions as subtle sex-drive killers. As the name indicates, they creep into the mind to obstruct mental perception with a sturdy impression of their own subject, to disturbingly create a deviation from various issues at hand… including sexual.

The contributory agents are mostly odors, some of which are offensive. Disconcerting odors include the following:

… Odor of food

All sweet-smelling fragrances and above all, the somewhat pungent ones from food items such as onions, garlic etc. should be avoided before sex. They create situations where the partner's mind switches back and forth between essential matters and food items or at times, food processing, ladies being regularly found in the kitchen. Additionally, sweet odors from food would become offensive in no time, due to bacterial actions; a change in value that's detrimental to all human activities including sex.

… Odor of sweat

It is pertinent to note that this odor is not that of sweat per say. Rather, the environment provided by the duo of body heat and sweat, being helpful for certain bacterial activities. In turn, bacterial activities will give off unpleasant odor. The more one participates in physical activities, the more should personal care be observed; that is, having a bath as quickly and regularly as possible… it will suffice.

… Halitosis/Mouth odor

This might be the *gentlest* of sex-drive killers: at all times keeping the partner one-step away. An average person is conscious of… and hence, ensures adequate personal effort on dental care, but this might not suffice. Recurrently, everyone would need a dentist for a comprehensive help. Mouth odor is repulsive and embarrassing. With the extent of physical closeness between couples during sexual intercourse, the incidence of mouth odor should be completely ruled out. It would be impossible for women recognized to possess high capability for sexual thoroughness, to concentrate on sex when her olfactory center is relentlessly telling her to step back a little. The exception is where the partner has a deficient smell center.

... Cologne

There'd be the need to keep the use of this product at a reasonable level if it cannot be avoided. There are tons of views in its favor, but there're contrary opinions against their usefulness as well. In any case, they might help to prompt physical closeness in a couple, at the early stage of sexual intercourse, when body language, fondly touch and romantic words are being employed as a prelude. The trick might be to spend an appreciable time on talking and foreplay generally, to allow the olfactory center become numb to it. Then its effect, as a source of distraction, wouldn't be much.

... Other odors

For foul-smelling and probably a deeply colored vaginal fluid, definitely couples will need to seek medical advice. The odor from the vagina should necessarily not be disturbing beyond that from an average man's penile/scrotal region. Meanwhile, there's an offensive odor that sometimes oozes from both men and women, when underpants are pulled. Personal cares have shown that this is due to trickles of urine that would inevitably touch the underpants after a discharge of urine. Additional contribution to this problem could be from sweat, as said above. To help reduce an offensive odor from this source, either partner should rinse the urethral orifice with clean water, each and every time they excrete urine. Noteworthy here is that women would likely smear their organ around the vulva, with more urine than men. Hence, they'd need to do better than the usual practice of just a dab with tissue paper after urination, by a number of women.

Using clean water, women should rinse the whole area within the *labia majora* before a dab with tissue paper. With this simple practice, particularly by women, such an unpleasant odor would vanish. And excluding infections, one would realize that it is possible, especially for a man, to wear his underpants for three consecutive days. Yeah! Three days and this under-garment wouldn't smell badly. Surprisingly, that of the woman too would smell clean for over forty-eight hours! And this is regardless of what medical viewpoint would consider as normal frequency of urination. Clearly, the man will be doing a whole lot of goodness for his wife, if he encourages her to rinse her vulva each time she expels urine. After a few days of observation, she too will thank him immensely for it.

At this point, it is appropriate to extend cleaning to a special part of the body… the anus. It's more relevant for people above age forty to go this far. Conversely, the effect of neglecting this seemingly small act progressively become pronounced on people when they're above age fifty. Above this age… human body muscles begin to sag, a condition known as sarcopenia; …also, it is more common for humans to break the wind. These and some other factors will regularly ensure the presence of non-abating fecal odor at the anus. To eliminate this odor, an easy and cost-effective approach could be achieved by regularly washing the anus with a mild soap and water up to twice… during the day. Of course, it is easier for women to observe this cleanliness. Simply, they could merge this special cleaning with the rinsing of the urethra opening… each time they pass urine. However, men would need extra effort to carry out this cleaning…. Commonly, the entire position adopted by men while passing urine will pose a formidable hindrance.

It should be noted that…:

> *… **A** rinse with water as a practice might become habitual, particularly for women.*
> *… **Using** the same under pant for more than a day is termed to be unhygienic; it is used here only to prove the cleanliness achievable when one rinses the urethral orifice with water after urination.*
> *… **The** description above has no reference to any religious or cultural practice.*

… Fingernails

This is not an odor, but undeniably a source that causes the greatest of distractions for women. Of course, the fingernail has a pain inflicting effect. Thereafter, the pain will distract her mind. Thus, the man should – at all times - keep his fingernails deeply cut short. Indeed, it hurts the vagina during foreplay, to cause an immediate diversion of the woman's attention; an undesirable situation in a gender that's particularly observed comparatively, as having the capability to display a longer sexual response. Noteworthy likewise, is the fact that the hands – especially the fingernails - are the major means of introducing bacteria into the vagina, during foreplay. From the activities of such bacteria, issues of offensive odor and vaginal fluid discoloration are the end result, although not exclusive. Therefore, the man is a major partner, contributing to the occurrence of repulsive stench, thickening and tinting of vaginal fluid in his spouse, via his fingernails. Of course, these are serious enough reasons for which to pay visits to a medical doctor.

Keeping short fingernails by the man is of considerable significance to an average woman. No doubt, this is the reason for which most women look at long fingernails on a man with disdain; they instantly perceive such a man as either not romantic or sexually… an illiterate.

From Adam to Eve…

Chapter 3

Applicable Skill

"Discretion shall preserve thee, understanding shall keep thee."

Proverbs 2:11 (KJV)

For some men, particularly those just going into marital life, to take a woman close to and watch her through orgasm might prompt their own orgasm. Then, it might be necessary to employ certain skills. Yes… certain skills do enhance sexual *activity*, but they are to be acquired and an improvement will occur only when such skills are continually put into practice. There isn't anyone who can lay claims to being born with fully matured sexual skills. These are abilities lacking in an average man that makes him sexually ignorant. Meanwhile, many of the products found on retail shelves, claiming possibility to enhance sexuality, are known to either increase the intensity or elongate the duration of sexual excitement, but with no effect on sexual skills. Physical sex tools are potentially perfect means by which anyone could prolong a sexual session, a concept that every woman is yearning for. But a foremost issue common to these sometimes-stand-alone products, include being artificial; they are never totally satisfying to an average woman. Another concern is that sex tools are yet to communicate emotional expression, a basic necessity in feminine sexuality. There is more on this in chapter six.

Remarkably, several types of pharmaceutical, herbal and nutritional products are excitedly sold both openly and in *black* markets.

They are products for which anyone could logically conclude that when applied, they'll inevitably require that the man must physically work assiduously, during a sexual contact. In an effort to procure consistent sexual satisfaction for the woman, these products would predetermine that the man must be overworked, each and every time he copulates with his wife. To start with, the requisite physical strength will nullify the possibility of making the woman attain multiple orgasms, and up to as many times as preferred by the woman. Second, overall physical exhaustion from the use of such a method will prevent the man from making a repeat performance as often as the woman can cope with. Funny enough, it'll likewise prevent a repeat performance as often as the man himself, wishes. Third and most importantly, the medical advice against the use of certain products in this category is due to established adverse medical effect. It is certain that multiple orgasms for the woman would bring her out of sexual passivity, and she too would desire sex as often as her husband. Of course, *the man wouldn't make his wife sexually active, only for him to plunge into inactivity owing to regular fatigue.*

If it is predictable that a woman will request for sex as often as her husband, it might be needless to beat around the bush; that special and popular counseling at marriage seminars wouldn't require elaborate caution commonly given. Then, emphasizing that a woman should not deny her husband of sensual contact might entirely become irrelevant. Apparently, the reason for the advice is to dissuade the man from seeking sexual delight from marital infidelity, to avoid ugly incidences that often stem from such actions. Stylishly here, the woman is being asked to use **sex as a tool** that could prematurely stop the man from marital infidelity. Truth be told, **if the woman herself isn't deriving necessary pleasure, she might be the first to look elsewhere for gratification.** Here's the process! Give as many orgasms as a woman requires and she'll come out of her shell in every way, in… and out of the bedroom, for her marriage. This book will attempt to lay out the entire what and how. Ultimately, it could end up becoming a marriage manual for every man. It'll show how a man will make his woman, over and over again, offer copiously huge sexual excitement sought after in extramarital affairs by virtually every man, to be directly available right under his roof. There'll be more on this in chapter eight. For now, to create the right flow, continue to serially… turn the pages.

The requisite sexual skills can be observed in an average woman; it's a portion of feminine sexuality and could be reproduced by any man. Possibly, the sexual passivity style of the woman could be responsible for deepening those skills, but the man should nevertheless, learn from his partner. Such skills will include the following:

… Remaining calm despite what he would see.

A woman would easily surrender to sexual disposition if her spouse is good with what to say and how to present it. She'd often give a subtle cue to pick on, either as a way to convey her interest in being led on or, as a response to the man's amorous incitement. The sight of such physical response could push a typical man close to the peak of sexual arousal. This speed prompting effect of feminine response is why the man should learn how to remain calm.

Foreplay itself comprises quite a few steps. The exciting thing – as said earlier - is that the woman herself will urge on her partner. This sexual input by the woman is more probable if the partner is wise enough to take a step at a time. This step wise action is an adventure most men would count as immaterial, but perceived by women as good sexual *performance*. However, instead of reading the woman's sexual language as… *move on to a further stage,* the man's mind will speed up into a greater pace. Usually, this dictate of the mind takes over and instantly, the man will rush into and through the foremost act. In this way, the most likely outcome is that the entire process will end in much less than two hundred seconds.

Other skills the man must learn, so as to be in control of the speed at which he moves to the peak of sexual arousal and hence orgasm, include the following:

…Remaining calm despite what he would hear, and…
…Remaining calm despite what he would feel.

It's obvious that what the man would need is some level of caution on how to relish what would excite him, much ability to control his senses of sight, hearing and touch. This inevitable control is what men would need to learn from women. As soon as any man perfects how to check each of this speed prompting *devices,* his spouse will perceive him as, "…A man," …to use a term commonly heard among women. Meanwhile, the ability of a man to subject these senses to control, apparently improves with age. Though, under certain other situations, it shouldn't be a surprise to observe the average man succumb to sexual exuberance, regardless of his age. This is often true when either the individual involved or the environment is varied. It's then clear that nature is in love and thrives better with highly varied settings. For now, the man would need to keep to the step wise approach.

Sex experts have identified four phases of sexual arousal in women: …excitement, plateau, orgasm and resolution. The knowledge of the first and the last two phases should suffice for a lay man; this'll take away complex academic exercise and pointless boredom from this issue. However, under normal settings, it is more prevalent to see the first phase eat up the longest time. It could take between a few minutes and up to one-half of an hour, or even much more, when the woman's sexual appetite is not asking for an expedite action. It is a sensual part that'll depend on a few factors which might include:

> …*How* well schooled is the man on feminine sexuality?
> …*The* woman's mood…
> …*How* deep is the man's knowledge about his spouse?
> …*The* extent to which the woman is prepared by the man, particularly, using words and…
> …*How* well the woman has been pulled out, into sexual activity.

It is notable that the first phase, known to last longest will be meaningful, if and only if the entire sexual session lasted long and vitally well enough, to ensure orgasmic pleasure for the woman. Otherwise, the ending resolution phase that's for relaxation… might often not be attained. It could be more appropriate to say that the woman will not go into the resolution phase; she'd remain somewhere within the excitement phase. Awkwardly, this differs from what's perceptible in men's sexual arousal. In women, it is a situation that could last for between a few minutes and up to several hours… until the woman's mind is taken up by other life niggles. As a matter of fact, the woman could recurrently, be in and out of intense sexual arousals for several days. It's a situation that could carry on for as long as her mind switches onto and off sexual dealings. Often, an average woman would camouflage this state of mind with pretense and an ugly perseverance while waiting for her man to go through his refractory period. Cogently, these actions prove that the woman did not go beyond the excitement phase. Logically, it's the very basis for sexual dissatisfaction. Meanwhile, to gain marital success, sexual dissatisfaction in the woman is a major issue the man would need to guide against. Therefore, what an average man should consider is that, (beyond how the woman feels while covering up intense arousal, the hope that builds up while waiting for future sexual attempts and, the state of her mind when sexual anticipations are repeatedly ruined) every wrong step will have severe consequences.

It's been substantiated by sex experts that men are easily aroused by what they see while conversely, women are easily aroused by what they hear. In the meantime, since a woman who's sexually dissatisfied would regularly go in and out of sexual arousal, such a woman could further be *hurled* into intense arousal by a man who knows what to say and how to put it. Then, via flattering, a man could noticeably perceive and then sexually exploit a woman who's intermittently going in and out of arousal. Erotic frustration lowers a woman's *guard*, making her a suitable punter for sexual advances. So, sexual dissatisfaction is what ultimately creates the period when a woman is unfortunately vulnerable to sexual infidelity. This is the time when pretense… the standard *tool* used by most women to conceal either their state of arousal or mental stress due to sexual discontent would most likely fail.

This is an aspect of feminine sexuality that's of course kept secret by women; …an aspect that should be respected by every man. This is for the fact that it's the root… which issues leading to resentment, emotional anxiety and up to feminine sexual infidelity in matrimonies, sprouts from. Carelessly, it's the aspect that's often misconstrued by most men as arduous and as being the result of excessive sexuality and sexual demand by women. Meanwhile, it is only an aspect that demands a little more, although not in terms of the man's physical strength, but skill. A skill by which several orgasms, in quick successions, should happen… and up to as many as the woman would prefer. Hence, one out of numerous questions that could be pertinent is, shouldn't the husband be held liable for his wife's sexual infidelity? Emphatically, the response should be obvious, considering the enormous amount of endurance a woman must have for her home to remain unruffled, while the inadequacy of her spouses' sexual response perpetually generates mental torture for her. Inevitably, this would be followed, by a buildup of anger and hatred.

> "Better…," the Bible says, "…is a dinner of herbs
> where love is, than a stalled ox and hatred therewith."
> Proverbs 15:17 (KJV)

From Adam to Eve…

Chapter 4

Favorable Trends

"…Behold, Isaac was sporting with Rebekah his wife."
Genesis 26:8 (KJV)

There's no doubt that oral sex is what some men use, to help obtain orgasm for their women or at least, get them aroused well enough. Oral sex is sexual action involving the stimulation of the genitalia of a sex partner by the use of the mouth, tongue, teeth or throat. Out of the two types of oral sex, Analingus and Cunnilingus, which could be applied by men on women, kindly pardon the scope of this book as it is limited to cunnilingus. Analingus, to an ordinary mind, would be a social aberration, feasible only at the lowest level of thinking; a detailed deliberation on it should be more suitable under a totally different book title.

As an aspect of oral sex, cunnilingus in the last couple of decades has had a significant level of appreciation among men, especially the youth. It has affirmative support from some of the research work that examined it from different perspectives. Then, starting with insightful reasons, men from older age groups and respectable social status are unobtrusively being lured into secret trial. This action is aided via a purposeful display by actors in pornographic trades and, as youthful enthusiasts' explicit expressions sifts into the public.

Therefore, apparent justifications for cunnilingus might include the following:

... As a part of foreplay

With the present level of sexuality awareness for men, foreplay is now an important aspect of sex, utilized not only to begin but sometimes to help in achieving orgasm for women. It's a feat that's more demanding during normal coital session.

... To accelerate feminine arousal

Ably, the tongue has been found to apply a good balance of gentleness and pressure on the clitoris. Clearly, this excitation is close to what's required. Then, it explains the high interest shown by women in cunnilingus.

... A way to speed up female orgasm

Really, every man wants to take his woman to the peak of sexual action. This is why expression that filters out from enthusiasts is able to motivate other categories of people, into trial. Accordingly, it is not a surprise to find men keenly craving to learn this new trick...

... To obtain a boost in masculine ego

With the use of cunnilingus, making the woman attain orgasm is found to be easier. Therefore, the man is thrilled by his newly found dexterity. So, from trial to regular use, more people are becoming enthusiasts.

... It is favored by a large number of women

Cunnilingus has a sexual method that involves the ***direct use of a biological tool*** by the man; an action that'll over and over again, urge a woman to crave for her spouse, and profoundly too.

A creative notion here has led to the understanding that foreplay, as a prelude to sex, could make men live up to their sexual responsibilities before the woman. Though, cunnilingus is helpful, it has raised both health and social issues. These issues have placed a clog into the process of its outright and immediate approval as a sexual mode to be encouraged by all, irrespective of cultural, religious and other inclinations.

It is a fact that women all over the world have common complaints, that...:

> *... **Most** men often do not ensure ample effort to make them attain orgasm during sex.*
> *... **Habitually**, foreplay is not sufficiently used...*

In other words, foreplay doesn't just stimulate women, it drives passion. Often, it is a pertinent precursor for sex, and if liberally used and prolonged, women would attain orgasm with ease by its mere use. In the meantime, it is regularly observed that a man would reach orgasm, much earlier than his spouse, with or without foreplay. In men therefore, foreplay only serves to liven up, but not vital for them to achieve orgasm, provided sexual dysfunction that's been known as existent at various degrees in every man, is favorably at a low level. Moreover, there're hints on the significance of foreplay on men, stated in the next chapter.

Therefore, these facts have revealed that men would need to perform foreplay on their spouse more than what they should anticipate. So, men came up with cunnilingus as a means that'd not only excite, but drive passion and most likely, take women to orgasm. Certainly, cunnilingus has proved to be fairly intense and able to do pretty much in assisting men. However, as in all situations, cunnilingus itself has adverse health and social issues which might include the following:

> *... **It requires** bending into a bumpy position for the man, leading to muscular stress and ache.*
> *... **It is** offensive to most men and as a matter of fact, some women as well!*
> *... **Cunnilingus is** not applicable in all situations, especially where evaluation of health risks may be unviable.*
> *... **It does** not allow a perfect usage of simplified sexual health safety measure. Experts say the use of prepackaged dental dam, or makeshift barrier such as a condom cut open, will only reduce but not eliminate health risks accessible via the use of cunnilingus.*
> *... **Cunnilingus is** a safer sex merely in the case of unwanted pregnancy, but beyond doubt, not a safe sex. Medical researchers have proved that several STDs comprising herpes, viral hepatitis, HPV etc., can be passed on through its use. The recent scary information by research professionals, that*

links oral sex to neck cancers, will bring about a second thought for sure.

… *It is* a sexual mode that no religious leader will publicly recommend from the pulpit.

… *While in* public, some men will shy away from divulging its use.

Deliberately, for health and social reasons, Cunnilingus is left out of foreplay in this book. Factually, it is used to augment men's sexual response; a practice that thrives since a better alternative is yet to be suggested. Besides, it's also deficient for the following reasons…:

… *It* cannot generate sufficient compression on the clitoris for potentially attainable excitement.

… *The* frequency at which one can tickle with the tongue cannot be varied efficiently to drive sexual pleasure to the peak attainable by women.

… *It* only allows an intermittent use of romantic words since the tongue will be busy.

… *With* cunnilingus, sexual delight obtainable by the man, as his spouse goes through arousal and orgasm, would be limited to that from sound. The man's face would be partially tucked away from the woman's facial and body languages.

… *Cunnilingus* can hardly be utilized to excite the woman further than one orgasm, owing to tension and ache on the collar and tongue muscles.

… *The* tongue cannot caress the clitoral hood, the clitoris, the *labia minora* and the vaginal orifice at the same time. This multiple caressing will require an amount of speed the tongue muscles can never generate.

… *Cunnilingus* is not applicable across all social and religious statuses.

Relatively, cunnilingus is blocking its own desired effect. A notable feature for *keeping the marriage healthy* would be deactivated. To have a *booming* marriage, sexual excitement is a reciprocal necessity; the input is essential and *partners will have to offer it mutually*. Also, couples are expected to practice the best health care. Dental dam and whatever improvisation that may be utilized by men, cannot be that safe. A grip on the vulva is not possible except where the barrier is worn the same way as underpants. Even with that, containing the feminine fluid might be unrealistic when the attempt on cunnilingus is to be sustained for a long period of time. When compared…? Women could try fellatio for two reasons. The first is because the protective barrier for men, the condom, is designed to have a good grip on the penis. Second and more importantly is that fellatio would be right, if and only if the lubricant on the condom is clearly labeled as, "safe for human to consume." Otherwise, the woman would be exposed to unwanted medical issues. Even where the couple has been together for donkey's years, all the same, the man should still be cautious for the sake of his wife's health.

It is necessary to avoid health problems during foreplay. Reasons for having sex do not include sharing terminal ailment like cancer with one's spouse. Therefore, couples might need to dump cunnilingus and devise better means by which men would pamper their women to a gratifying sexual pinnacle. Hence, certain other substitutes could be considered, to replace cunnilingus and probably, oral sex in totality. These substitutes might include:

… *Affection mixed with humor.*
In and out of bed, most women need what goes a little beyond sex, often with a step-wise approach. In the right mix then, the use of affection, humor and romantic words, on the basis of their separate effect as mental stimuli, will open up most women for sex and should be utilized.

… *Patience mixed with passion.*
Except when she's rearing to go, in every sexual session, women prefer a gentle start, followed by a gradual build-up.

… *Sexual self-confidence mixed with dexterity.*
This is not about bragging, but telling the woman about knowing what to do, when to do it, how skillfully it would be done and possibly… what's to be achieved.

… *Tenderly touch mixed with appreciation.*
Instinctively, women can pick on the most covert of sexual expressions but they prefer and are delighted by verbal and overt ones. Talk about and be plainly fond of all her feminine and sexually nice body features.

… *Specially handle erogenous zones.*

A woman being lucky with more erogenous zones is not an issue to them. Rather, they are simply better at relishing sexual excitement. A man ought to be active with his fingers and must not briskly sprint across foreplay into sex. The more a man stays on foreplay, the easier and quicker will it be for his partner to attain orgasm. Meanwhile, those erotic zones peculiarly observed to be more active in a woman, proffer a romantic avenue that could be extensively used…

… *Fondle with affection.*

Typically, most men do this as a prelude to sex, but women will also show appreciation for its use when sex is not intended. The resourcefulness of a woman is doubtless…. She uses this step and the previous one in two ways: …to create and serve sexual zeal if in the end, she's successfully pulled out of sexual passivity; and as stimulating means to induce her man to savor sexual excitement.

… *Pick on subtle cues using special ability.*

Men should keep their minds tidy as the woman's sexuality isn't immoderate. The affectionate tendency by a woman is a special creation by God. It's a tool for specific actions that'll create sexual excitement for her man. For obvious reasons, the woman will tuck this tool away from a man who knows little about feminine sexuality or, who doesn't know how to bring his woman out of sexual passivity. All the same, she'll make use of subtle cues so that her man could kick start her show of affection. The ability to pick on and utilize these subtle cues will bring her to the level where she'll cautiously unveil not only feminine sexuality, but schooling her man further about her personal sexuality in particular.

It is a common feature to find men frowned up when in public with their wives. Whereas, when a woman is kept smiling and happy – in and out of the house - she'd also be easier to open up for sex. For women, an initial focus on non-erogenous areas will stimulate the brain. This will get the sensory nerves around the erogenous zones ready for excitement. Helpfully, a preliminary focus on non-erogenous body parts will avert unpleasant tickling, when erogenous zones are eventually caressed. Meanwhile, the use of substitutes to replace cunnilingus – such as in the last seven steps - would create simultaneous excitement for relevant senses and the brain, generating a greater outcome in a shorter time on the woman. In flourishing marriages, couples enjoy substantial *sexual excitement* in addition to the unique pleasure from sex itself.

It is conspicuous that pious men who walked and worked faithfully with God also employed this technique. They knew that caring for the woman would make her perform matrimonial roles, in or out of bedroom, with greater efficiency and intent.

Here's how Holman's Christian Standard Bible (HCSB) puts the idea…

> "… Abimelech king of the Philistines looked down from the window and was surprised to see Isaac **caressing** his wife Rebekah."
>
> Genesis 26:8 (KJV)

From Adam to Eve…

Chapter 5

Being Factual

For we can do nothing against the truth, but for the truth.
2nd Corinthians 13:8 (KJV)

There's no married woman in her right senses, who'll ever treat issues about masculine sexuality with a wave of the hand. She'd simply be pushing a hot knife through the *heart* of her marriage. Every man will agree that these statements are true, no doubt. If this is so, then there's no reason for the converse statements not to be absolutely true. If there's an agreement on this, then, it is imperative that men should search for additional methods to unearth information on feminine sexuality. Clearly, by the time an average man is fortified by this further knowledge, he'll get to know his shortcomings. Then, the question about having inherent capability to perfectly cope or not is an issue on which special inference would be made by everyone, before the end of this book. But in the attempt to obtain this essential information, there'll be the need to pry into a path most people might classify as unpleasant and maybe decadent.

So, regarding feminine sexuality, men would need to extract certain strategies from the view of lesbians. This is not a backing for this act. There's nowhere in the Holy Bible that supports lesbianism. Hence, Christians must never in any way, back homosexuality in whatever form. Meanwhile, as detailed in second Corinthians chapter thirteen, eighth verse, Paul cited that, "We can do nothing against the truth…." The truth will forever remain true regardless of where, how

From Adam to Eve…

or why it is being used and, who is using it. Hence, here and in the entire contents of this book, there's the intent to further cling to the flawlessness of the creator, God Almighty. Therefore, nose-poking into lesbianism is basically an approach to identify what's of immense benefit… the truth.

> "Acknowledging of the truth…"
>
> Titus 1:1 (KJV)

It is plain that lesbianism is being incited partly by men's big letdown. Accordingly, some women turned through one hundred and eighty degrees, and away from men, to obtain sexual delight from persons of their own gender. Lesbianism is a complex notion that does not conform to logic. The practice itself is in conflict with well-known social and cultural practices the world over. These conflicts are the very reasons for which open and intense criticisms are regularly raised by cultural and religious groups. Such criticisms explain why women who are into the practice would hastily point out concern over societal rejection. This is an issue that could have been needless if the practice has evident progressive effect on social virtues. Definitely, the practice is scientifically clumsy; it is clearly inapplicable to marital purpose for procreation. Besides, it's a practice that lacks relevant entities that'll consume the utility of a woman as detailed in Proverbs 31, verses ten to thirty. It is obvious that lesbianism evolved from secret acts. A clandestine situation where a woman deploys profound feminine sexuality to obtain sexual pleasure from another woman will absolutely expose masculine sexual flaws. Apparently, some women have made use of not just words but what could be perceived as a decisive and complementary action as well. Thus, a rather soft inference is that lesbianism is a blatant expression by some women to convey absolute turn away *from men's low sexual response*. Then, the idea of lesbianism depicts a group of women who are making assertions which might include the following:

> *… **They** know a better way out of the mire.*
> By chance, they have learned and are expending a means that offers the best opportunity to show sexuality in accordance with their personal desire. As such, sexual pleasure is provided for… or obtained from one another and, to whatever depth they so desire.

48

... It is a break to avoid a non-abating endurance.

Some women are no longer willing to continue to put up with mental ache; they have been utterly thwarted by an unfortunate sexual response from members of complementary sex.

... Courage is vital in every development.

They are bold enough to rise up against what they considered as not sexually favorable to them... from men.

Lesbians make the most of the following steps:

... The vital head-on sexual technique

This is a technique that'll allow both partners to be fully involved in sexual activities. In addition to the use of words, partners will ably use eyeball communication and free hands to caress, to further excite themselves. Here, it is possible to posit an act of foreplay by lesbians.

... Simulation of the primary act

Precisely, there's a situation where a partner could be said to be playing the role of a male. Then, it is possible to presume that sexual intercourse is being simulated. This'll include a situation where the *masculine* mate is making use of an artificial penis or any other tool on the partner.

... Fulfilling partner's sexual desire

This is an aspect that needs no explanation; of course, it is where Lesbians are ever so thorough.

Notable in each of the above steps is the fact that lesbians are gentle and never in a hurry. So, from the perspective of lesbianism, issues about feminine sexuality requiring vital consideration by men will include the following:

...Physical gentleness.

...Sexual confidence and thoroughness.

...Satisfactory duration, attention and dexterity.

With regards to feminine sexuality, these are basic facts that should never be ignored for whatever reason. Passion for these features is innate and so, in perfect compliance with aspects of feminine physiological paths that cannot be altered. On a second thought, an average man offers these features but at a shallow level nearly every woman abhors. Luckily, these are sexual features anyone could see to in two steps or so… using foreplay.

Beside reasons for its demand by women, foreplay has gratifying effects on men as well. Therefore, hints on the impact of foreplay on men may include the following:

> *…The man* will relish erotic delight while giving pleasure to his spouse.
>
> *…Essentially, after* an extensive foreplay by the man, the most apparent follow-up is a reciprocal action from the woman. Predictably, such an input would serve to calm the man and in the long run, help him stay longer on the primary sexual action.
>
> *…Greatly caring* for a woman's sexual aspiration will bring her out of sexual passivity and in turn, she will provide extensive foreplay to her man, to snowball the preceding importance of foreplay.

It is now clear that anything short of an ample masculine sexual response will adversely affect the woman. In a situation where the man is in addition, being insensitive, he'd absolutely be defrauding the woman. In the end, she'd become angry, irritable and tense, and in silence, sexual infidelity could creep in. On anyone including women, sexual frustration could create multiple openings via which negative ideas could sneak into and ultimately, smash the marriage. And in due course, the man will *grow up* to understand that he… shot his own foot.

The Holy Bible confirms that couples must never treat issues about sexuality with a casual attitude. It'll bring about a perfect opportunity to switch on a time bomb for that marriage by… of course the special character known to everyone; …a force very much formidable against any marriage, anywhere.

> "Defraud ye not one the other, except it be with consent for a time, that ye may give yourselves to fasting and prayer; and come together again, that Satan tempt you not for your incontinency."
>
> 1ˢᵗ Corinthians 7:5 (KJV)

Chapter 6

Naturalness

"Likewise, ye husbands, dwell with them according to knowledge…"

1st Peter 3:7 (KJV)

Procuring orgasms for women via unnatural methods, might involve the use of sex tools. Often, men regarded the mode as unimportant provided orgasm is obtained. However, regardless of the technique used, the act would undeniably be followed by feminine appraisals. Then, the difference can only be interpreted by the woman. As a matter of fact, if this effect is solely emotional, certainly, it should be expected to be massive. To a good extent, procuring orgasm for a woman via an unnatural mode will require that she'll have to drive arousal with a deliberate effort, same as it is in masturbation. On the order hand, during the prelude to an orgasm via natural means, the notion of arousal, pleasure, passion, etc., will all follow an effortless natural passage. For a fairly detailed insight, there would be the need to take a cue from another source that's clearly disagreeable and later, facts could be stringed together.

Of course, commercial sex is where the idea of arousal, passion, pleasure, love etc., are not of prime importance. Indeed, it is a community where the female commercial sex worker has a totally different intention for engaging in sex. As in all businesses, the commercial sex work is nothing but a money-making endeavor. It also boasts of popular strategy like client satisfaction, which afterward may dictate the price. So, the notion of feminine passion in commercial sex, if at all required, could also be price driven; it'll of course, be bundled into the *sales'* package. Thus, commercial sex work may be made to conform to a deliberately manipulated sexual activity. Most likely in this way, sexual act will not flow from the mind as expected. Moreover, it could lack the divine and graceful effect of rekindling love. Consequently, the sex worker could use the next available sex implement or surrender herself for a twisted and offensive sex, once the transaction is sealed and payment made.

In a situation where a man's sexual response is grossly deficient, his woman might make use of sex tools when anxious for orgasms but most likely, it will be in the absence of the man. It isn't that she cannot use it in his presence but she'd naturally want to divert or at least set a safe limit to the thinking of her man. Predictably, she'll want to prevent a wild and wrong impression about her sexuality and that of women in general. Consequently, an unfortunate circumstance will take root. In this situation, an average woman will… more and more, withdraw from marital exuberance to become gloomy, lonely, tense and resentful. Each of these emotional states will form tons of barriers against sexual excitement in the home. Together, they'll blend and within a short period of time, grow into the natural precursor for marital infidelity and indeed, for either partner.

In the commercial sex industry, that special aptitude in women with which they could create sexual excitement for men is a plus, supporting effort to boost patronage. Mere expressions of arousal, passion, caring, etc., that could most likely be bogus, are mixed with some amount of indecency. Deliberately, these tricks are regularly used to drive masculine sexual enthusiasm to the peak of motivation possible. As at that time, social decorum and norm would be of zero meaning and hence, all cautions would be thrown to the wind, to satisfy a client. Extensively, they'll exaggerate and utilize feminine sexuality. Tactically, this attitude is meant to fashion the opportunity to pull in additional clients; hopefully, they might expertly convert more men into future customers. Frankly, this stimulation is a key impetus luring-in potential customers. It is also the factor that's urging regulars, to make their covert and often nocturnal patronage more repeatedly.

As a source of generating immense pleasure for men, this livelihood is second to none. Believably, it is the oldest profession after farming and most likely, the occupation with the shortest financial break-even period. If such a profession is brazenly opposed to social, cultural and religious views in every society, then, something must be absolutely odd about it. Therefore, it shouldn't be a surprise that after a desertion of this trade, the female commercial sex worker is seen as in need of help. At that moment, she'll not be taken to a hospital for a medical cleanup and of course, not to a bank manager, to consider a new business. The very first place she'll likely be helped into is the office of no other, but a psychologist. This assistance would be an endeavor to salvage the state of her mind that would be recognized by now, to be subnormal to that of an average woman. By implication therefore, prostitution is seen as not being in conformity with the societal view of the feminine nature; …a nature that's believed to be divinely endowed with moral uprightness. About a woman in such a trade, the conviction is that she's either enticed by its economic prospects or forced into it by social problems. Then, women in commercial sex are mentally considered as not being *women* any longer and, anyone who decides to renounce the trade will definitely require the expertise of a psychologist.

Sincerely, it is compulsory to make an apology for these expressions. They are not meant to castigate anyone in the trade. The statements had to come up in an attempt to describe the fact that such women perceive themselves as being in business. They are out to make money and have simply set up a business with minimal resources. The target is optimum value when input and earnings are compared; a fact that's valid in all businesses. Also, it's an assessment that's common among business executives. With the exception of health risks, it is a trade in which the fiscal break-even point could take place on the very first day of business. Certainly, this is a highly desirable yet uncommon feature in the business world.

Meanwhile, the psychological effect of orgasm alone on both male and female has been liberally documented by sexuality research experts; a recap isn't necessary. It'll only be fine to add that the average woman prefers when orgasm is procured via natural means. ***This preference is crucial and should not be ignored.*** To buttress this fact, research observations have shown that the natural mode for sex, popularly called the missionary style, is the favorite for most women. In this mode, the fact that it will no longer be necessary for the woman to consciously drive arousal using her sense of imagination will confer a whole world of liberty. If orgasm or more appropriately, multiple orgasms, are achieved in compliance with the woman's preferred method, she'd regularly succumb to sexual desire. In this way, she'd seek sexual intercourse as relentlessly as her man. Furthermore, she'd decisively use top level feminine ingenuity to nurture the level of sexual delight for her man; she'd have been hauled out of sexual passivity.

Straight away, there seems to be a link between orgasm and a glowing splint of love. It's a fact that a man must reach orgasm before he can procreate since ejaculation of his semen coincides with his orgasmic climax. For that reason, every sexual intercourse ends in ejaculation for him. To avoid confusion, it is relevant to point out that this book is not discussing procreation, and ejaculation will hence not be discussed beyond what is mentioned above. For this book, the major subject is how to have a successful marriage and briefly, valid factors will include all inputs that are of protective relevance to a marriage: love, caring, commitment to partner's development, etc. For an exhaustive list, one should go for a quick browse of the Internet, on the reports of related research topics. What is of relevance is the insight and contribution of sex and precisely, orgasm to whatever list anyone might scoop. Meanwhile, sex and orgasm *profoundly, are the toughest of suitable mortars for affection.*

So, straight away… after orgasm, the man would have reaped massively and he'd move on with life. Soon afterwards, when the man's refractory period would have elapsed, perceptibly, all his language forms would communicate renewed fondness for his spouse, with the desire to relish from another sexual excitement and orgasm. This desire should be expected because each sexual act contributes an overhaul of enthusiasm for the woman in the man. At that point, the man must have reflexively, absorbed a rekindling of dedication for his wife. By a divine fate, the woman is the one enabling orgasmic process for the man and for this reason, the man keeps coming back, with a refined (or is it a *renewed?*) emotional state. Then, an involuntary rejuvenation of love must be repeatedly occurring for the man. Likewise, on a regular basis, the woman notices every expression of affection emanating from the man as he climaxes, thereby pleasuring from the fact that she's giving him pleasure.

If the man could make his wife reach orgasm in the same way, equally, the woman too should be expected to come back for more. As a result, the woman would seek sexual pleasures as often as the man. Likewise, and significantly too, there's no way the woman will get to orgasmic climax without the man also relishing some pleasure, forming a reciprocal situation similar to the picture in the preceding paragraph. That is, the man too will receive pleasure also by giving pleasure. Here, what's of relevance and worth stating, is that this reciprocated action of giving pleasure will inevitably, result in mutual rekindling of love and commitment between couples. This is the best way to improve that major and most dynamic of the forces that provide strength to that strangely complex bond between married individuals. Recurrently, this mutual glee from orgasm will enliven the tendency of this bond to be cohesive, to pull… and to balance every affectionate occurrence.

Thus, from the exhaustive list previously mentioned, this mutual orgasmic delight will invigorate each item on a regular basis and in turn, they'll recurrently enliven the attraction of the love bond to remain cohesive. Surely, this is a major feature that will support couples to weather the storm of marital exigencies with remarkable ease. Absolutely, it is equally capable to quell much of emotional whirlwind of life, along social and economic lanes for either partner as separate individuals. Also, it is pertinent to mention that in all of these situations, the woman as a complete epitome of higher capability compared with the man, has requisite ability to aid the man to further perfection as specified in Genesis 3:16, "And thy desire *shall be* to thy husband." Divinely, she is wired to know and deploy the high level of communication that exits in all of these situations to support her man and at the same time, safeguard their romantic union. Undoubtedly, this is why there's a steady preference for the ***masculine tool***…. To incorporate sex tools, the man would do better if he would first of all, learn copious amount of romantic expressions from his woman.

In the meantime, the last part of Genesis 3:16, "And he shall rule over thee," compels the man to be humble in his *role* as he strives to ensure marital success. To gain some insight into this, again, it would be needful to dig into the same disagreeable source for facts. Obviously, there'll be the need to know how an aggregate of sexual excitement for either of the partner and feminine sexuality revolves and interact. Likewise, it will be necessary to identify what attendant effect would such an interaction have on the inputs that are of protective relevance to a marriage and ultimately, marital success. From the pry into the commercial sex industry, it could be presumed that women are conscious of facts that may include the following:

…The significance of feminine sexuality.

Undeniably, feminine profound sexuality is inborn. It is a special physiological aspect created by God in a woman, to serve a special purpose. Although, the control lever is with the woman but she'd often prefer that the man is the motivator, as he leads on. Then, the purpose for feminine deep sexuality will include a way to *help* the man in his search for marital success.

…Purposeful usage of sexual excitement.

Sexual excitement enlivens gladness between a man and a woman. In a marriage therefore, it will help in charting the path to marital success. In contrast to this purpose, women in the sex trade use aspects of feminine sexuality to excite clients craving for sexual acts. Here, the anticipation is to improve on potential returns. Nevertheless, it is a misuse of a powerful heavenly gift in a way that's totally opposed to the calling of a woman. As a wife and mother, the woman has simultaneous roles that should guide everyone in the family into a lifespan of happiness and success.

…Poor sexual awareness in men.

An average man isn't aware that a woman loves to devote every aspect of playfulness to her man. That is why she is able to differentiate between **play** and sex. Perfectly, an average woman is able to gear sexual excitement in whichever way she desires, either to rekindle love, craft sexual delight or both. However, an important role here is that the man and not the woman should start off the process. If a man starts off the process of sexual excitement, effects that will emanate will include the following:

> …***Consciously*** or otherwise, the woman will come out of sexual passivity to create sexual delight for the man.
> …***The*** mutual pleasure that'll ensue would further bind aspects of love, and tuck away stress emanating from other life endeavors, to lead the couple to marital success.

Evidently, the usage of sex tools will be a sure way by which men could extend sexual sessions. Helpfully, sex products found on retail shelves are useful in ways that are exciting to both male and female. However, the woman is created to play certain Godly fixed roles. Naturally by this divine commission, the woman is guided to deploy **feminine sexuality, sexual excitement** and other features. These are features requiring human mental activity. Habitually, they are utilized by women to rouse delightful emotions in men. Meanwhile, expression of emotion is a distinctive medium of communication by women…; it is used to give and to demand marital vow from men. However, a major issue is that sex tools cannot converse emotional expressions. This flaw is precisely why a woman will forever find it difficult to replace a man with a sex tool. Therefore, in situations where a tool would be used, the man should know that he's the one at this point needed… irrefutably to bridge the gap.

The awareness of this situation is inborn in a woman; it is natural. However, she'd prefer to keep mute for the fact that an average man has a wrong notion about feminine sexuality. With greater ability to envision romance from pertinent angles, this is one of the reasons for which the woman will desire a relationship in which the man will be wise enough to make the most of her Godly endowed ability. Therefore, the man must learn not just the usage of sex implements when needed, but to simultaneously convey genuine emotions, to bridge feminine preference for naturalness and orgasm in his spouse.

From Adam to Eve…

Chapter 7

A Humble Role

"...Give her of the fruit of her hands; and let her own works praise her in the gates."

Proverbs 31:31 (KJV)

Thank goodness the situation is not totally gloomy. This is for the fact that femininity is not masked in ambiguity. Biblical teachings and information that filters out from other religions are also exceptional references, indicating the fact that the woman is a wonderful creation of God. As a "Help meet for him," Genesis chapter two verse eighteen, the woman is skillfully made to be a suitable helper for the man. Also, from the words of Genesis chapter three... verse sixteen, "...Thy desire shall be to thy husband," she's also directed to supportively act in this role without any prejudice. Using a second look, it would be observable, the world over, that most women carry out these obligations with absolute merit. Hence, the woman will not discard her relationship, romantic or any other, apart from situations where she's been made to reluctantly become hostile.

Hostility is common to every human under mental stress, particularly when the stress is as a consequence of social and economic issues. Definitely, the so-called developed countries are not left out, but in these environs, deliberate steps are frequently taken to stem social-economic mess. However, in a developing country, imminent stress from the same issues is sufficient to cause emotional failure.

Nevertheless, regardless of how terribly low is social-economic deterioration in a location, yet, women would preserve their homes. So, more often and of course, more than the man, she's willing to help lower anxieties in the family. The woman is always willing to go as far as the use of humble means to get a little more on the table, glaringly, to augment her man's effort. Thus, this implies that the woman's roles are vibrant, daring and of course, clear.

With this clue, a major issue that needs reflection now is the expected role of the man; an excelling role that most men usually misconstrue. Basically, this is where there'd be the need to exploit honest and clear moves. It is where a man will have to take practical steps, to be more familiar with his woman. In this way, the probability that desired objectives will be accomplished using minimal effort will be very high. This is not about placing the man's role in an obscured perspective, but in the other way around. Without an iota of doubt, this book should place every man right on their excelling role, getting desired results not only repeatedly but efficiently too. Oh yes, the target is to reach a status where the woman will constantly be proud to refer to her man as manly. Certainly, this is a goal that is not as difficult as it seems.

An on-the-street marketer uses jokes to gain the attention of potential buyers out of passers-bye. In his endeavor to slow more people down, he made a remark which to his mind… is a humor. At the topmost level of his voice, he said, "those women who claim they have to put up with marital stress in order not to jeopardize their children's life and development, are not being candid." Thereafter, he concluded that, "If a man's libido is hyperactive, up to the point of death, his spouse will certainly tolerate anything." With caution, it is important to entirely avoid vulgar words used by the marketer, words tactically used to convert the larger part of unhurried passers-bye into an impromptu crowd. Of course, his throng chuckled and the trick in actual fact, worked. The marketer's product is though obvious, but of greater impact are his crowd-pulling and face-brightening expressions. Really, it was a joke but rational, and men could utilize the knowledge that is embedded therein. In three steps or so, thoughts within the marketer's jovial call could be unveiled using the perspective of an average man who'd like to be Godly.

Godliness at times, is a viewpoint for which some men are impatient. However, it is the means by which desired purposes could be effortlessly achieved. The wisdom in the marketer's expressions is for the fellow whose libido is hyperactive to identify that… he is the reason for which his spouse will not consider a divorce. Besides, that he has a rare opportunity to easily make his own… a marriage of reference. Factually, to naturally prolong a sexual session is an ability that's not obvious and particularly, a rarity in men. However, to ensure this all-important marriage of reference, the man will only need to take simple steps more. In these steps, the man would need to… avoid rivalry in the home, ask for… and often make use of family inputs from the woman, let the woman share in his success and finally, show gratitude to his spouse… on a regular basis.

Up to different levels, these are guidelines already being observed by most men. Of course, these are expectations that are frequently observable in every woman and distinctly, right from dating. In a marriage, any man that'll observe these rules will be very close to becoming his spouse's kind of man. Most likely, he'll be half way through to meet up with her hopes; the other half will come from his "hyperactive" libido.

… *Avoid rivalry.*

In a romantic relationship, a man should not take up the position of the *boss*. Honestly, an average woman is often wittier than most men, especially on issues of family and romance. Despite being wittier, she's neither envious nor hostile to the masculine ego. Since she's unruffled about the man's self-esteem, a woman will ensure her romance is intact. As a result, a woman wouldn't purposely upset her man up to the point of debilitating his ego. She has an aptitude higher than that of the man deliberately made by God. Rather, she'll habitually desire to offer support of a "help meet" to her spouse. Women have an innate capability to love and to provide moral backing for their men. With these virtues, they're perfectly in conformity with the divine order that says…:

"…Thy desire shall be to thy husband…"
Genesis 3:16 (KJV)

Women married to men regarded as public figures go through a huge task, to boost their husbands' self-esteem on a regular basis. This feminine input is more visible when the man is getting ready to attend a public function, and regardless of her presence or not at the event, she'll ensure a befitting and honorable outing for him. She'd delightfully aspire to do so and very well also. Typically, irrespective of the man's social status, this situation will be found to be the same. In a family having financially low status, the woman in addition, will undergo mental agony in secrecy, in her effort to make certain that there is no fiscal clog up while acting out her divine roles. This **desire to her husband** is why a woman is choosy about whom to date. She's carefully searching, certainly not necessarily for a rich guy, but a man that'll relentlessly crave in addition to showing appreciation for… her support and friendship. So, with greater capability to envision romance from all pertinent perspectives, the woman will desire a relationship in which the man will be wise enough, to make the most of her divinely endowed ability.

… Let her offer family inputs.

By the time God decided to create the woman, He wanted a being with remarkably higher qualities, and *in favor of* the man. That was why He stated that Eve wouldn't just be a trivial partner but *a help* that would also be "Meet" to Adam, hence endorsing a perfectly appropriate associate. As a result, the woman is a perfect and divinely suitable companion for the man and precisely, that was why God said…

"…It is not good that the man should be alone; I will make him a **help meet** for him."

Genesis 2:18 (KJV)

Usually, it is the man that'll woo the woman into dating and courtship. Although, the woman might make the earliest move; however, trust women, they know when to stealthily turn such situations around. Physically also, the belief is that a woman is living with her husband but in spiritual terms, it is the man who lives with his wife. Despite all of these and some other beliefs that are probably interpreted falsely too, the man has a firm desire to be *the man of the house.* Thus, he'd nurture all applicable fiscal muscles to house and train his children. Nevertheless, the woman is very much higher in qualities required to build the family!

What every man wanted, is a crucial philosophy that's obvious; …to have the greatest family and to evolve the best romantic relationship. Ably, the man has the power to comprehend and work for what he desires. For this reason, he's willing to use inner determination and extensive vigor that is second to none, to achieve his intention. However, to achieve this effortlessly, the man will simply need to co-opt his spouse. She's got the necessary qualities to further refine his method. The labeling of the man as the head of the woman is precisely why he must have basic humility. He needs to take up the role of someone who will habitually tap into his wife's mind.

Therefore, what everyone would be able to figure out here is that the man has the requisite aptitude. He's the one to look for essential resources that'll be used to build a family. In the meantime, his success will be with the assistance of (and kindly take note...) *an ably eligible and divinely made helper*... the woman. However, it is unfortunate that where most men often go wrong is in their attempt at doing it all single-handedly. They work so hard using all they've got, but with their lips shut. Even if it's not acceptable to all, a fact will remain unalterable. Thus, on family sociology and related issues, the woman is created to have a couple of *steps* ahead of the man. Hence, as an appropriate "helper," she is properly qualified not only to advice but to also offer exceptional input when and in whichever way the man is deficient. Men would need to pardon the use of the word... *deficient*. It is improper to be hash with words but caution is being taken also not to renege from the promise of being frank. Possibly, the use of... *in need of assistance* would be a better expression. Meanwhile as a suitable partner, she'll not only come up with feasible ideas but will also be eager to see that whatever honorable idea her husband decides to adopt, converts essentially to success.

An unfortunate reason, for which much of family inputs from women are frequently left unused by men on the dining table, could be traced back to the directive found in sixteenth verse of Genesis chapter three. Here the Bible says, "... And he shall rule over thee." This is a Bible section that has remained grossly misconstrued by most men for several centuries. Buttressing this wrong notion is the thinking that the creation of Adam before Eve, is in line with the order of superior-to-subordinate direction; hence, the view that Adam is a higher quality being to Eve. In countries where English isn't the mother tongue, "... *Rule over you*," could rigidly be interpreted as... *boss over you*. Besides, it could be described using a master-slave relationship. These analyses no doubt, are entirely wrong. A humble reasoning about Genesis chapter three, verse sixteen is that it is intended to further demand for compliance with the purpose of Genesis chapter two, verse eighteen, "...I will make him an help meet for him" (KJV). Since the order at Genesis chapter three, verse sixteen was made after the fall of Adam, then, all the feminine abilities within Genesis chapter two, verse eighteen will be wrapped up and utilized in Genesis chapter three, verse sixteen. As a result, the directive, "…And he shall rule over thee," could be rephrased as, *you shall – regularly - use your help meet capability to support your husband*. Somehow, this relationship between Adam and Eve is similar to that between joint proprietors in a modern business enterprise where partners, due to distinct skills, handle different but complementary jobs. It is a situation where partners input will be mutual while the intention is to safeguard their business' success. So, Genesis three, sixteen really clarifies that woman's input is meant to guide marital union to success.

The woman is a unique companion, with the capacity to offer suitable assistance to her man. Small wonder her reactions often portray mixed feelings of disappointment and frustration, whenever the man becomes excessively bloated with masculine personality. Undeniably, the woman is convinced that the man's ego is the leading issue that makes him not to perceive unreserved necessity to obtain assistance on household affairs from his partner. It shouldn't be a surprise that the woman could be accurate…! Where anxiety stands possible is with a man who steadily wears the habit of control over his wife, at times, with a hash and sternly attitude. Nonetheless, regarding masculine ego, women grasp nothing at all, to contend with. In that case, it could be that they are always delightful to live in accord with the role divinely given to them. The woman… as stated in the twenty-seventh verse of Proverbs chapter thirty-one, is ever ready to boost her man's capabilities, to ensure success in the "ways of her household."

"…and worketh willingly with her hands"

Proverbs 31:13 (KJV)

… Let her share in the man's success.

In Proverbs chapter thirty-one, from verses ten to thirty, the Holy Bible itemizes the qualities of a virtuous woman. It confirms that she isn't only hard working, but capable to handle multi-tasks. Nevertheless, what is of paramount significance is that men should take a closer look at the very last verse. Proverbs chapter thirty-one, verse thirty-one is being directed **not** at the woman but the man. It says…:

"Give her of the fruit of her hands; and let her own works praise her in the gates."

Proverbs 31:31 (KJV)

To understand the first part of the verse, "Give her of the fruit of her hands…" the choice of words by The Holman Christian Standard Bible puts it in simple and clear terms by saying that the knowledge within the expression is, "Give her the reward of her labor…" The man is directed to be fully aware that his wife is a part of him, she should be allowed to share in successes that may accrue, and side by side with him.

…*Acknowledge Her Inputs.*

In the later part of the verse that says, "… and let her own works praise her in the gates," there should be extra scrutiny to reveal more knowledge therein. The author of this book is neither a native speaker of the English language nor a student of literature. Therefore, tons of grammar issues will hamper his effectiveness. Hence, every effort would be made to stay out of language technicalities, even if that is what would bring out relevant points. Hence, readers would need to pardon this evasion. Very briefly therefore, "…And let…" would be a way of saying …***by a deliberate effort, the man should allow…, (never hold back on…,*** to use a stronger term) *explicit commendations or open displays of the woman's contribution to his successes, whenever there's an opportunity for such an exposé.* Also, to ***let her own works praise her in the gates***, the Bible is buttressing the fact that the man should let the effect of the woman's effort be publicly visible. Simply, the man should be proud of his woman's inputs. Praises and expressions of delight are moral incentives; the woman would be motivated to nicely offer more for her spouse. Surely, this pleasant offer from the woman would make the man's earnest intention to evolve a successful marriage and a peaceful family an easy task. Befittingly, when a man gives credit to his spouse, that feminine nature to support the family will encourage any woman to give more. With an unreserved input from the woman, ***the man would become exceptional among his contemporaries and in his endeavors***. An astonishing aspect to this is that she'd aspire to do more and very well too, regardless of her man's financial status. This candid support is a unique quality that cannot be taken away from a typical woman.

From Adam to Eve...

From these four steps, there's a clear idea about how the man could take control of his romantic affairs. Via divine intuition, these are basic steps every woman expects from her man. When taken regularly, these steps would reduce friction between couples. These are steps that could be referred to as *the golden rules for a successful marriage*. Regardless of the number of factors that are of protective relevance to a marriage, scooped from the Internet as directed in the previous chapter, each of the items on such a list could be ordered under a particular one of the four golden rules above. Any factor outside these four would be categorized under the fifth rule. Conspicuously, there are five of them, forming *Five Golden Rules for a Successful Marriage*. The fifth one will come up in a later chapter. When these golden rules are not followed, a woman would perpetually wear the feeling of dejection in her countenance. Gradually, dejection would build up into anger, beyond which the woman could painfully quit a relationship. When the four rules above are closely used, the woman would be pulled more closely to her man, loving him more and of course more open for sex. It is then that overt sex moves would have the expected effects on her.

Thereafter, the concluding and perhaps *a foremost step to becoming the manly man would be easy to take*. It would also be possible *to move that pace as far as expected*, for the couple to profit from its natural purpose to the fullest, making it obvious that it's a step that would be taken in two parts. It's a major step, embedded in what could be called the fifth golden rule for a successful marriage.

> *No doubt, Proverbs chapter thirty-one verse thirty-one, "Give her of the fruit of her hands; and let her own works praise her in the gates," (KJV) is a very significant Bible verse. It teaches an extremely important knowledge that should be made known to men, at every marriage seminar. For the sake of emphasis, this exposé should be made before, during and after all that's needed has been said and done. The right meaning for this verse is not common or maybe thus far... the verse is perceived as irrelevant. Plainly, it comprises all complementary implications that could be inferred for verses ten through thirty... to give the qualities of a virtuous man.*

Chapter 8

Uncovering a Scheme

"Finally, brethren, whatsoever things are true…; think on these things."

Philippians 4:8 (KJV)

When it is time for physical and emotional pleasure in a marriage, the cursor on the family agenda most likely, will be pointing to sex and sexual excitement. Sex and particularly orgasm, that is expected to climax a sexual activity, is what gives the greatest physical and emotional pleasure known to man. In most marriages, the woman is often passive sexually; she'll endlessly wait… expecting her man to step up sexual delight in the home. So, she'll have to endure sexual discontent. With time, the woman would become vulnerable to dishonest sexual advances from outside her wedlock, owing to unfulfilled sexual desire in the home. Unintentionally out of mental stress from lack of orgasmic pleasure, she too will send sexual invite signals to every appealing member of the opposite sex.

Likewise, due to sexual passivity in the woman, the man will not enjoy significant level of sexual excitement from his wife. To begin with, he does not understand how to create sexual excitement that could regularly take his wife to desired orgasmic heights. To live up to this task, he'll turn himself into an ancient steam engine; he'll make use of either unsustainable techniques or products that'll compel a laborious exercise. These are techniques and products that will soon be abandoned, to send the woman further into her shell. Ultimately, he will look outwards, ready to pursue greater sexual excitement from somewhere else. By this time, sex in the home would become boring. Then, other supportive factors such as… the relative ease with which men could have sex with no strings attached; …a greater opportunity to frequently change the environment, etc., the man will get lured farther away from his wife. However, if any of the **away matches** should last a little long enough, he'll gradually fall back to the same sexual moments that will – in no time - **bore the woman concerned into fury.** Essentially then, this inevitable occurrence is a proof that something is wrong… definitely not with the man, but his technique.

In the meantime, for not offering necessary assistance to the man, wouldn't the description of the wife as a *help meet* make her culpable? Wouldn't the man misconstrue intentions of sexual ideas from the woman, when such ideas are offered without hesitations? Isn't a marriage in this situation doomed to crash? And… who should be the appropriate person to make the first move in an attempt to salvage the situation, and how…? Of course, with this kind of back and forth jumble, isn't someone being negligent, ignorant or both?

Honestly, the man should be blamed for all these clutters. From Biblical standard, he is the head…. In clear terms therefore, he's the one who should convey the intention to avoid matrimonial failure. Of course, in his choice to wed a particular woman, he would have marital success as one of his objectives. Then, he must have seen a path that could lead to his marital anticipation in the chosen woman. As the head, it is obvious the man must collate essential resources… including his "**help meet**," to build a home. Sincerely, the process of building a home is a Godly conduct that is inborn in everyone. Hence, no man would consciously be biased in his decision to have marital success. Then, the man shouldn't be weary to take just one more step, to realize his marital objectives.

Of course, it is irrelevant if the woman made the first *move* to start off dating. Likewise, who's to be dissuaded from the first *move* into marital infidelity – the man or the woman, is of absolute irrelevance. However, since the man didn't leave "his Father and mother" for the sake of nothing (Ephesians 5:25 to 31), then, it is his duty to lay down his intention to achieve marital success. Hence, **the very first step against marital infidelity must be taken by the man.** This statement cannot be over emphasized, and henceforth, men must allow it to reverberate endlessly in their minds. Then, a pertinent question that could crop up is… ***what knowledge would the man need to fine-tune, if he is to ensure marital success?*** The response to this question is within the contents of this book. Additionally, concrete effort to string these steps into amazing results would be revealed in the next chapter.

More than any other marital issue, sex contributes more reasons for which couples split. In African communities, a common inference is that, "Couples will not own up on core reasons…" for mediators to relevantly resolve their marital conflict. One and all will play down on important issues. Sex – couples' most probable reason for conflict - should not be deliberated upon in the open. As the head, ***the man should be the first to think through the idea of sexual contentment in his marriage.*** He should be the first to ponder on how to ensure sexual delight for his wife. At the beginning, sexual excitement and not sex, is a foremost step that will prepare a woman's mind for that very sensational delight that's able to rejuvenate conjugal union. Once the woman's mind is ready, she'd evidently respond to all obvious sex moves her man might offer. Explicitly, she'd urge him on as well. For a woman, this step that could lead to sexual intercourse has a purpose. Mainly, the purpose is… ***hope for sexual satisfaction*** for women. If we could poke our minds into marriages the world over, this is the step that'd be predominant in well over 90% homes. The step consists of where the man is only able to achieve a low level of sexual satisfaction for his spouse. Of course, from what would be obtained from this book, this is a low-level *performance…*

Clearly, the fifth golden rule comprises two parts. Within the paragraph before this one, is the first part. The second and probably the major part, is where the man must use the skill that'll create sexual satisfaction for the woman. Such a skill must ensure that women truly profit from sex, in the same way as men. This is the step that could make any marriage an ideal romantic relationship, in the face of sexual and non-sexual issues tugging marital roots. Somehow, contents outlined to guide this step… could turn this book into a marriage guidebook that's second to none.

Due to seemingly greater sexuality observable in women, there's the need for men to know how to make up for the obvious gap. (At the end of this book, every man would be able to ruminate and infer, if their wives had greater sexuality or, they had been ***working*** at a level that's far below man's inborn amazing capability). At present, the need to close masculine-feminine sexuality gap has made modern scientists to develop various methods to improve sexual activities in both men and women. Though, it is noteworthy that additional effort, if not all, should be channeled towards *how an average man could achieve a better sexual response.* Definitely, sexual issues would be better resolved when tackled from men's viewpoint; most of the **issues tugging the roots of nearly every marriage could be linked to insufficient sexual response in men.** To annul this apparent gap in sexual response, every man would need to understand basic knowledge about orgasm and its uniqueness in women. It is a crucial knowledge and its usage would help bring any woman out of sexual passivity. When a man is able to **pull his woman into sexual activity,** the whole world of sexual pleasure would open up for either partner. In particular, the woman would be offered what women naturally and covertly crave… a sufficient and excellent sexual life. Inevitably thereafter, there'd be a very high prospect of having a joyful matrimonial life. Dr. Oz, a respected and famous medical expert in the USA says, "If you want to have a **fulfilling, long-lasting** romantic relationship, then, sexual intimacy should be of utmost importance." Fairly, from whatever perspective this statement is considered, it is the truth. If this is so, it will be inevitable that orgasm, an occurrence that specifies the peak of sensual desire, should certainly have a role to play.

Typically, the incidence of orgasmic pleasure for men in every sexual session is likely; it is predictable. Masculine orgasm is generally known, but it is a condition that's commonly untrue for a woman. Hence, pertinent question should be …how could men guarantee regular event of orgasms for women, by the same token? Similarly, isn't it significant to emphasize that any man who considers this issue with levity should be prepared to face marital disaster in whatever shade or magnitude. Undoubtedly, an insufficient level of orgasmic pleasure for a married adult is a nerve wrecking situation. It produced unending emotional concern in our grandmothers. Cruelly, it made single parents out of most of our mothers. An enduring worthwhile romantic relationship will require inputs from both partners. In addition, it will demand a further logical input from the man. If sexual interaction and of course orgasm, have all the benefits explained by relationship experts, then, women also must necessarily be made to savor orgasmic delight as frequently as they prefer. Since the woman prefers to turn to her spouse each and every time she's seeking sexual gratification, then, it is crucial for the man to search for a simple and stress-free method to accomplish this obligation.

The most common feature is that once a man achieves the first orgasm, he'd need to unwind. He'd chill out over a *refractory* period. Refractory period is a length of time that varies from a few minutes in some men who are extremely lucky. It could extend to several days in a number of others. If sexual intimacy is sufficiently deep and both partners' communication is of a good level, then a man would likely have the desire to help his spouse achieve sexual pleasure. Recurrently, he'd take her to the peak of sexual satisfaction. Certainly, a regular attainment of orgasm is significant to the woman; hugely, she'll gain from sex and orgasm, in the same manner as her partner. However, lack of regular orgasmic pleasure for women is made difficult by no other reason but men's low sexual response. Logically, this predicament is made worse due to an inflexible outlook by most men, when a woman attempts to offer a helping hand.

In a media article, a lady made an anonymous disclosure that once she's had an orgasm, she'd have the feeling of being revitalized rather than that of exhaustion. This is a simplified manner by which an individual could describe the tendency toward multiple orgasms. At that moment, if the source of excitement is sustained, that woman will achieve a second orgasm. If this source of excitement is sustained long enough, the woman will achieve further orgasms; the ability to show the occurrence of orgasms in multiple series being inborn in women. Somehow, the disclosure by this woman is a point strong enough to validate the idea that women are aware that they have no refractory period. Certainly, this exposé bares feminine sexual stunts! It's the aspect men find difficult. As such, most women will be swift to admit that **men will persistently misinterpret their sexuality as excessive**. This offers a distinctive reason for which a woman will ignore the idea of helping her man to improve on his sexual response. As a result, she'll hide underneath sexual passivity. Subtly and skillfully, she'll veer off each time the subject comes up. She could go as far as not talking about feminine orgasm at all. Undeniably, most men are living by this dummy, due to a low-level knowledge about feminine sexuality. If sexual dullness should persist, in no time, she'll blame the man for being sexually insensitive and perhaps… see him as a sexual illiterate.

Research experts have proven that refractory period in a woman is either extremely short or totally absent. This evidence clarifies the capability of a woman to achieve a number of orgasms in quick successions, an idea that's referred to as multiple orgasms. Unquestionably, it is the level at which an expression of feminine sexual reactions will have a reduced censorship. Also, it would be easily observable that when a woman is made to attain multiple orgasms, clearly, she'd have... and exhibit more of sexual contentment. Therefore, if multiple orgasms are factual and could only be experienced naturally by women, then, this experience must be the level at which they'll greatly profit from sex. Since it is this outstanding benefit from sex that will give the feeling of sexual satisfaction, at that point, it would be a feeling that women or anyone for that matter, wouldn't be able to hide. ***Remarkably then, a similar level of benefit obtainable by men in one orgasm would logically be accessible by women, when they're made to achieve multiple orgasms.***

Up to now, men have tried to boost sexual performance using one or a blend of some of the following...:

...Physical body exercise
This is perceived as good because there are tons of concepts in its favor, particularly on its positive effect on human health.

...Dietary products
These products should be acceptable for the fact that they are dietary and hence are expected to have reasonably lower adverse effects on human health.

...Herbal/Pharmaceutical products
These are special products that interact with body physiological processes. Thus, there is confidence that a developed mind will make sure that they are recommended by a medical expert, who will be sufficiently capable to weigh the risks that could be involved.

...Sex implements
In recent decades, sex toys are products that have gained and increasingly receiving approval among couples. Where exceptions could be found might be among couples from countries with low social-economic and possibly too, low academic growth.

...Skills in oral sex
Certainly, cunnilingus is getting more admiration. It is an aspect of oral sex that has been found by some men to be rea-

sonably effective. As such, covert remarks from such men are inspiring some other men into its use; cunnilingus has an amazing capability to pull in more fans on a daily basis. However, for some men to put their lives at risk while trying to sexually satisfy women is full of surprise. Beside diseases already linked to vaginal sex, cunnilingus could place the man within more health risks.... Via the use of oral sex, the list of sexually transmittable diseases is incredibly long. Reliably, cunnilingus would be a perfect sign that men are secretly having a massive anxiety over imaginary shortfall in their sexuality.

So, if there's a technique by which a man could help his spouse achieve multiple orgasms on a consistent basis, the best would be to make use of it. This usage would be apt, if the mode is not intricate, preferred by women, and not laborious to men. Under these conditions, any man would be able to perform beyond women's expectation. A man who performs sexually beyond the expectation of his woman will forever be treasured by that woman as caring. Joyfully, she'll always refer to him as manly. In the meantime, whatever method by which the man will offer multiple orgasms to the woman should additionally have the possibility of pulling her to him. Such an option will require that the procedure favored by women must be given the greatest preference. Commonly, this option is the man himself and not the use of sex toys. However, if any sex implement is to be utilized, the man should get ready to – first of all - justify, and to personally use them. Thus, a woman's mind would still picture turning to her man for sexual fulfillment.

From research reports, "sexual intercourse and orgasms trigger oxytocin to be released into human bodies. This hormone is what gives couples the sensation of being remarkably fused." Oxytocin is therefore tagged, *the love hormone*. In the meantime, a global research institute has shown that when a woman is lacking sex, she'll have the feeling of distress, but the lack of emotional connection is much more hurtful. Obviously, due to the fact that a sex tool is inanimate and unable to generate emotions, it wouldn't be the first choice by an average woman who needs to create mutual sexual delight. She has a perfect knowledge that sexual glee will foster partners' closeness and ultimately, marital happiness. Furthermore, research has confirmed that women do far less of sexual fantasies than men. Then, the simple inference is that women more than men, have greater preference for *natural biological processes.*

When a woman is regularly taken to the peak of sexual pleasure by her man, an emotional connection should be expected to proceed from such a woman to the man. The feeling should be expected to be substantial when orgasm for the woman, is obtained via her mostly desired sexual method. Remarkably, emotional connection is a dynamic component in romantic relationships; it has a tremendous refilling energy that's meant to sustain the relationship itself. So, before the decision to choose sex toys, it seems a man should get to know not just how it works, but the opinion of his spouse as well. In the succeeding chapter, there is a little more on emotional component… and how it could be sourced.

To reveal a better scheme, there'd be the need for men to think about what would be required in generating sexual satisfaction for women. Without doubt, any man who is thinking about offering sexual satisfaction to his spouse must never look down on foreplay. So, whatever sexual technique that might be proposed must live up to certain conditions. Such conditions might include abilities to…:

…Keep foreplay as an essential aspect of sex.
The method that could be proposed must include foreplay as a part of its process. Thus, it will have in-depth ability to start off deep sexual glee for men and women alike. Where desirable, it should aid attainment of orgasm by partners, especially the woman. A technique that will retain foreplay as a vital part of sex will thrill any woman.

…Make foreplay sexually exciting for men.
This will make men to be part of the excitement obtainable from foreplay, just like women. Surely, this will nurture masculine attention in an aspect of sex for which most men are impatient.

…Amplify feminine sexual excitement.
The method should offer a veritable approach to hasten up the attainment of feminine orgasm.

…Widen sexual period without fatigue.
Absolutely, this is what every man should look for in sex toys. Nevertheless, if armed with a sexual method that'll provide this instance, skillfully, the man will be able to keep his spouse at the peak level of arousal. Then, such a method will

ensure the attainment of the desirable feminine orgasm and surely, in multiple successions too.

...*Meaningfully boost the masculine ego.*

Surely, this will create the feeling of diligence in the man. This feeling should be expected because the man will regularly make his spouse attain orgasms with ease.

...*Inspire couples' interest in mating.*

Communication, both verbal and non-verbal, is a tool the woman uses throughout the duration of every sexual action. Deliberately, it is directed at raising sexual delight for the man; particularly, this is why women will choose frontal sexual mode over any other. Thus, any sexual technique that'll allow the use of facial contact for communication will be women's ideal style. It will encourage the woman who'll in turn thrill her man, and in the end, build mutual sexual delight.

...*Be in conformity with social views.*

A suitable sexual method shouldn't only excite the youth, if it complies with social decency, it is what leaders in various fields of endeavor will equally commend and endorse.

...*Be in conformity with religious views.*

Irrespective of creed, a sexual method that every religious leader will endorse, even from the pulpit, will thrill everyone.

...*Show compliance with medical views.*

Indeed, the ordinary man is far below conviction that he could *perform* impressively and beyond feminine sexual expectations, without the use of products that'll boost sexuality. A sexual method that'll prove this and at the same time, conform to medical advice will certainly be an eye opener for men.

...*Be workable regardless of size.*

A prevalent concern both in men and women the world over, is being anxious when body or genital is of a small size. Then, a sexual method that'll be feasible, irrespective of these overt anxieties will confer a whole world of relief.

...*Help foster logical and focused expenses.*

While most women will accept sex toys purposely to nurture playful spree and hence couples' closeness, most men will pursue them as sexuality heightening products. These are distinct ideas which if fused by a suitable sexual mode could ensure mutual excitement.

From Adam to Eve…

…Preclude unwanted issues.

A sexual mode shouldn't just be better… it'll be more acceptable when physical contraception could be employed, if and when desired during a sexual exercise. This'll help prevent sadness associated with having an unwelcomed baby or STD.

Once armed with a sexual method that'll capably satisfy the above conditions and perhaps some other pertinent ones, it's most likely that every man will have a good report in his nuptial life.

Chapter 9

A Simple Logic

"Let love be without dissimulation... *Be* kindly affectioned one to another...."

Romans 12:9 & 10 (KJV)

Somehow, ideas have been dotted in bits and pieces in earlier chapters. Certainly, what the author has avoided is the daunting exercise a non-native speaker of the English language will face, if these ideas are to be placed inside a short, four-hundred-word write-up. Meanwhile, as soon as a man is able to effectively seam these ideas together, the woman will hope for special sexual acts that should end in orgasms. Then, arousal in the woman would have been encouraged up to an appreciable level. It isn't that women are difficult to arouse, but a man must learn the peculiar method that'd quickly lead to sexual arousal in his spouse. Effortlessly... as said earlier, women would get aroused via the use of romantic words. The next step would be to take this arousal level in the woman, a little further. Often, this further stimulation is seen by men as unnecessary but it's over and over again, favored by most women! With practice, the man will get to identify what will aid his effort. However, what's notable is to ensure the woman will not perceive a tickling sensation at early stages. When tickling is experienced by the woman, the man should know that he must have either disregarded or skipped some important steps, which habitually include the use of romantic words.

From Adam to Eve...

Steps for additional arousal could include the following. Kindly let's create the scenario for a man that's a right-hand user. Any man who's a left-hand user would need to use the other side of the bed and, thus reversing the positioning here described.

...Let the woman lie by the right side of the bed, that is, with her right hand close to the edge of the bed, the left will be in the middle.
See figure one below.

Figure 1A

Figure 1B

The next four steps could be adapted to comply with own methods that would easily arouse the woman. Where the couple is young, learning or just trying out new concepts, then the method here specified should be tried; it is very simple.

…Comfortably, kneel down beside the bed. The situation is the same if the man prefers to be on the bed; this step could be performed while both partners are on the bed. Either side of the man's body could be turned to the woman, depending on personal preference.

Note that women would prefer a situation that'll favor facial contact for obvious reasons. Thereafter, the use of a slight change in positioning, interchangeably, would be for the avoidance of monotony in the woman. Moreover, to change from one position to another would equally be found to be necessary in order to vary the tempo at which to perform and especially, to avoid numbness.

…With the mouth placed over the breast, fondle the nearer nipple with the tongue and lips.

…Stretch the left hand to… and fondle the farther breast and nipple as regularly as possible.

In the meantime, as said, the man would need to make deliberate effort to know and regularly make use of what will excite the woman extensively. Note that at the early stages of arousal, most women will slightly conceal their feelings, subjecting their arousal response to deliberate control. With sufficient intimacy and sincerity, ask and she'll mention the position and touch that seems best for her. In situations where it's the preference of the woman that the last two steps are taking in the reverse sense, then move on to her left side on the bed. The two nipples may possibly not create equal level of erotic excitement for her and as such she could have a handling preference. At some other times, she might dispel handling preference as inessential, due to human complexities!

…Gently move the right hand around, to caress the pubic region. Occasionally, the hand should be pulled up to fondle, more like a support for the nearer breast, while the tongue is on its nipple. It could also be used to fondle the other breast while the mouth is on the nearer nipple. Equally, while caressing the pubic region, occasionally use the middle finger to tap, time after time on the *labia majora* such that the effect could be felt around the clitoris. Ensure gentle but firm touches with both the tongue and the fingers.

The last three steps may be performed for a period that's up to a quarter of an hour or more before an attempt to move on to the next step. Where these three steps have yielded results, she'd have positioned her legs slightly further apart, wide enough for the middle finger to get to the clitoris. Specifically, do not go after the clitoris yet. This further widening of legs might be her direction for the man to go further…. Nevertheless, it might also be an expression indicating the point of entry into the mood for sex. If this widening of legs is an expression of entry into sexual mood, she might experience tickling feeling if the clitoris is touched at this time. Such a sensation is a sign that the man is hasty, moving at a speed that is too fast or he's missing important steps. So, the moment her legs are spaced out, change from tapping the labia majora to patting on it, using four fingers. Do check to know if she is sufficiently wet and if the clitoris no longer gives her a tickling feeling. At that point, move on to the succeeding step. If not, continue to pat on the *labia majora* and combine this patter action with the use of the last three out of the five previous steps. With much care, do not rub on the clitoris and any part within the vulva when she's not wet; this will not only bruise her but could terminate the sexual session at that moment. Here, it is noteworthy that the hand the man could use more skillfully should be the one placed at the pubic region.

…With the finger that could be maneuvered most easily, which probably is the middle finger, spread her vaginal fluid; cover the entire area within the *labia majora*. Really, do this as often as needed. Also, cover almost the entire length of the middle finger with her fluid.

…Place the right palm on the pubic region. With the middle finger, recurrently tap and tickle on not the labia this time, but the clitoral region.

…Continue to tap and once in a while, tickle the clitoral region. Ensure that tapping is at a regular rate, start slowly then gradually increase the rate. Afterwards, gradually ease into a situation where patting the clitoral region could be performed with two, later on three, and finally four fingers… in a way she'd find easy and suitable.

Fingers should be introduced, one at a time. The purpose for this is to carefully avoid drawing away much of the woman's vaginal fluid on to the large surface area of the man's fingers, within a short period of time.

…The moment it becomes convenient to pat with three or four fingers, push the third and the fourth fingers slightly forward, as if they're being braced from behind by the index and the small fingers. In this way, patting will be more proficient, down to the clitoris. While patting, a more effective impact could also be accomplished if the clitoral hood is allowed, every now and then, to push slightly in between the third and the fourth fingers. In the meantime, spread her vaginal fluid now and again, to cover as much area as possible. Likewise, use the occurrence of fluid-smearing, to directly tickle the clitoris as well for some time.

Allowing clitoral hood to poke through two consecutive fingers, the straight pat and the tickle, are ways to vary the stimulation, to avoid monotony and numbness on the woman. Simply observe the woman and maximally use each of the stimulations, changing from one method to another when it becomes necessary. In addition, spend a longer time on the stimulation that creates the most intense excitement.

Up to the last step above, where each step had been taken properly and slowly, some women would have had an orgasm or two. When multiple orgasms are not in the plan, the couple could begin sexual contact. However, if copulation occurs at this moment, and the man achieves an orgasm, the masculine sexual desire would have been satisfied, most likely, well above 95%. In the meantime, feminine sexual desire, after one or two orgasms, perhaps would have been satisfied up to somewhere above 20% but certainly, far below 30%! The woman's sexual desire could have been satisfied a little further, if she was made to attain one or two more orgasms before the beginning of intercourse. This additional experience is significant; it is often required by women. Getting the woman one-half way into sexual gratification might require that the man should make good attempt to extend the duration of sex a little more.... Then, the woman could be getting between the third and the fifth orgasm, at a time not too far from the first one.

As a reminder, the aim of this book is to let men know how to **naturally** make women achieve orgasms between ten and twelve multiple times before an intercourse! This will ensure that the woman will…:

…Gain from sex and orgasms.

…Radiate reciprocal pleasure to the man and,

…Create regular sexual delight and marital bliss for the man, all through marital era.

Obviously then, the humble skill is yet to be elucidated. To even get to this level, a good percentage of men will covertly employ one product or another to boost sexual act. Meanwhile, it is apparent that a larger percentage of men may not perform beyond the level so far discussed, even if the opportunity to utilize sexuality enhancement products is absolutely, thrown open by medical experts. In this book however, there's much surprise for a man that cannot make his wife attain an orgasm without the use of products meant to boost sexuality. An orgasm…? No, the shock is for a man who's unable to make his wife attain regular orgasm in multiple series as desired by the woman, and without an iota of exhaustion! An additional surprise here is the capability that's inborn in an ordinary man. What could bring about obstacles for any man are conditions of ill health, particularly erectile dysfunction.

Where erectile dysfunction or loss of libido is suspected in any way, the best option is to consult a medical expert. Sexually related health concerns are beyond the scope of this small book. Amazingly, they are more common than what anyone might think of; sexual health issues exist at different level of occurrence in practically everyone. As a matter of fact, sexually related health issues provide more than enough reasons for which every adult should do regular medical checkups. Sexually linked health issues are reasons for which a large fraction of men from developing countries indulge in impulsive self-medication, and particularly, the ingestion of unrefined herbal products.

Chapter 10

Hope for Satisfaction

"Defraud ye not one the other…"
1st Corinthians 7:5 (KJV)

It is obvious that the nine steps in the previous chapter are intended to prepare the woman for a normal sexual contact. Therefore, sexual contact is possible at the end of those steps. However, if the intention is to give multiple orgasms to the woman, then, the man should not go for an intercourse yet. This is the stage at which most men err. Surely, the woman would have been ready, and most likely, she'd have had an orgasm or two if the man was able to properly carry out the nine steps above. By now, the woman could be eager for a move on to further steps. Hence, she could physically tug but undoubtedly, via actions, urge on the man…. This is to direct the man to move on to the next step, which is the use of the penis. For now, the man should not use the penis but romantic words to calm her down a little. If this is the first time the man is offering multiple orgasms, he'd need to make his intentions known. Basically, the woman — at this moment - would need to perceive extreme sincerity in the man, particularly about his aim. To have an easy job, a prior chat about it will do a whole lot of good. This is no suspense but a careful attempt to have **salespersons with requisite skills, in the attempt at selling cold water to ice-makers**. Undeniably and irrespective of masculine perception, the fact remains that women were created to be better than men in all aspects of sexuality. However,

From Adam to Eve...

this book will uncover how an average man will use this superior feminine sexuality, for his woman and marriage to benefit from.

Beyond doubt, a man will not have personal experience with which he could describe the incidence of multiple orgasms in-depth; it is an exceptional aspect of women's biological processes. Somehow, a woman who has never had more than one orgasm in a sexual session will know that a second one isn't far away from the first. She might not even have words to describe it but the concept surely is feminine.

On the incidence of orgasms, clarifications by pertinent professionals found in libraries are deep and explicit. For the man, the professionals' description is that arousal is easy and rapid. Within a short period of time, the man is ready for sexual intercourse. Meanwhile, the moment he attains an orgasm, it is highly likely that his high level of arousal would also be rapidly lost, as long as the man is not acting under the influence of any product meant to boost sexuality. He'd then need to wait for some time to recuperate. Likewise, to have interest in another orgasm would require his body's Biology to *build* the need from zero level up again.

Hence, men experience what experts refer to as refractory period. During this period according to the free internet encyclopedia, Wikipedia, "…Men would notice a mental feeling of being sexually satiated and at that moment, are not interested in sexual activities." Some men, depending on individuals concerned, might remain in this situation for some days. Similarly, immediately after an orgasm, the penis would most likely, become hypersensitive for a period that may range from a few minutes up to a couple of hours. During this period, the man will perceive sexual stimulation as unbearably tickling. So, during the period when the penis is hypersensitive with its attendant awful tickling sensation, how sexually enthusiastic could a man be? Likewise, what could be the effect of feeling sexually satiated; isn't this a feeling that'll **escort** a man into and through his refractive period? Using these thoughts, it is apparent that men would exhibit the tendency of being dissuaded from having several sexual sessions in a series. Thus, if multiple sexual sessions are closely packed, the chances for a series of up to ten orgasms to take place in a male (if rationally possible) will be unbearably slim. The chances that a man will have up to ten orgasms will even be much slimmer, if the scenario comprises a single sexual session having its duration suitably extended. And so, we could presume that normally, **men do not**

have the ability to experience multiple orgasms. This is masculine and no one has been able to change it, at least up to now. At any rate, the virtuous thing is that this book will show how to use the short period of sexual intercourse, being what men can afford, to accomplish the best result. Also, it'll describe how this short period of sexual intercourse could be extended incredibly and suitably for the woman to attain between ten and up to twenty multiple orgasms!

For women, experts' clarifications are totally incredible and of great significance. According to the same source, Wikipedia, "***Women do not undergo a refractory period after an orgasm and in nearly all situations, they have the ability to reach additional multiple orgasms through further stimulation.***" The insight is that sexual arousal in a woman is gradual and builds up at a slower rate than it is in a man. At the end of the day, when she achieves the first orgasm, a woman will virtually stay for a while at the peak of arousal. This is notable and it is what every man could and should exploit. If erotic stimulus in a way, is applied beyond this extent, the absence of refractory period would lead a woman to continue at that moment, to relish sexual excitement and certainly, more orgasms.

While describing personal experience in chapter eight, the lady that made an anonymous disclosure in a media publication, also referred to a sexology research report when she said that, "***Men are said to feel sleepy after an orgasm, but rather, she feels more energized.***" In reality, this must be a factual occurrence in women. Precisely, it is a different way of describing the concept that women would wait for a while at the peak level of sexual arousal. Thereafter, arousal would begin to wane, and incredibly slowly too. This distinctive feminine behavior, at the level of sexual climax, is a solid reality that's been validated by results from aptly relevant research works: medical, social and others. Effortlessly, simple observations could be applied to ascertain that these relationship experts are particularly accurate. Of course, this typical behavior is as a result of physiological activities happening inside the body of the woman, and somehow, it is an incident that could be detected using a simple logic. This simple logic by which anyone could observe the effect of this amazing biological process would be stated later on.

Meanwhile, research experts have shown a large number of benefits obtainable from sex, too many to go through in this small book. Specifically, ***sex is said to be a good emotional component in a romantic relationship.*** This is an excellent benefit, but isn't orgasm what is generating the needed emotion, while sex is a natural procedure for achieving orgasm? By some means, some might say this statement is another way of emphasizing the point made by research experts. However, a logical outlook would be the fact that, **when a man fails to help his wife achieve orgasm as and when desired, obviously, the woman is being deprived of that emotional ingredient.** Inevitably, such a woman will lack one of mental stimuli needed in every romantic relationship. In romantic affairs therefore, sex and… mainly orgasms, are occurrences of protective outcome to the existence of the relationship itself on one hand, and the lives of married individuals on the other. This welfare should be expected, when either partner is helped to savor the outstanding benefit obtainable from orgasm, to moderate life stress.

Physiologically, women are made to experience multiple orgasms while men are normally expected to be satisfied with just one. Then, it would be easy to conclude that *the physical and emotional benefit realizable by men in one orgasm… would require multiple orgasms in women.* So, when a man helps his spouse to attain multiple orgasms on a steady basis and as regularly as she desires, she will reap enormous benefit from sex. Thereafter, her love and devotion to her man will grow to an extremely high level. Essentially then, multiple orgasms would be in line with women's body physiology. With respect to this feminine nature, it might not be totally wrong to agree that women are conscious of their desirable sexuality. What men need to be attentive to is why women are never emphatic when they need to gratify their matchless biological desire. As a matter of fact, this knowledge should regularly be used by every man as an index, when trying to carry out his bed-top obligations. Well, kindly pardon the diversion from the subject of the chapter.

From the last step above, the man especially the young, inexperienced and new in the *business*, would need to be cautious. No harm is meant. The caution here is not to jump hastily into sexual intercourse as the woman also could start a request for penile sex. This is an act the man must refuse using romantic words. Insist on and continue with the actions in the last four steps, in order to achieve the intention. Tell her to savor the excitement. If this is the first time the man will attempt this exceptional treatment, really, the woman will lookout for sincerity before she'd allow him to continue. Her major reason for caution here is that she'd reason that the man will perceive too much of **feminine profound sexuality**, an incident she wouldn't ever want misconstrued for **excessive sexuality** on her part. At that point, the man should get ready for women's typical bogus defense that, *"Orgasm isn't a necessity for women…"* This is a well-rehearsed speech, so commonly heard that one could conclude that it must be available in every culture on this planet! So, the man must gear up for this gimmick; it is highly likely she'd throw it at his face, to discourage him from making any additional effort.

When the intention is to make the woman attain multiple orgasms, the man should move on, from the last step in chapter nine, to the step below…:

> …While she's still in the same relaxed position on the bed, sit down and use the bodies of you both to form the letter 'L.' The man should sit between the woman's legs, in a way that her legs should be crossed over his legs and placed beyond his body. The man should have his left leg kept on the floor, while the right should be beside the woman on the bed. In this manner, the woman's body would've been located between the man's legs if he were to place his left leg also on the bed.

Figure 2

It is noteworthy that the man may not find it comfortable if both of his legs were placed on the bed, (See Figure two). In an attempt to go into this position for the first time, the man might need to convince his woman using romantic words. He would need to watch out, most likely, she'd be staring directly at him, making every effort to determine his aim, to see if his actions were backed by sincerity. In this state, every woman would weigh sexual experiment and sexual excitement on a psychological scale in an attempt to know if her man's intention is on the basis of love and care. Therefore, she'd subject every action and words from the man to mental scrutiny.

The woman is mentally alert and romantically informed; hence, she'll persistently measure the man's actions, in a stance to monitor and check wild guesses. It's one of the ways the woman protects her marriage. Probably, women believed that a misconception of feminine sexuality could thrust their romantic relationship into a dangerous yet preventable whirlwind of conjugal glitches. Thus, the decision by the woman, within a few seconds, would determine whether or not she should fabricate an excuse with which she'd prove the irrelevance of an orgasm for women in general and for herself in particular. However, once her decision is not favorable, promptly then and there, she'd nullify the exercise and the man may wish himself better luck at some other time.

Even if she's convinced, the woman would still be wary. Thus, she'd offer a partially hindered access, tentatively allowing only a small extent for the man to maneuver. During romantic chatter, the man's sincerity and tactful use of romantic words will combine with feminine sexual arousal nature. This will help the woman in not just getting aroused, but to give the whole idea a greater drive within her thoughts. Then, it is most likely that the first attempt will be successful. Hence, subsequent attempts would be captivating. Figure two above depicts the positioning for all the steps pertinent to multiple orgasms.

Chapter 11

Focus on Caring

At the first time of taking a woman through multiple orgasms, the man may perhaps, need to pass through the stage of persuasion. The procedure will be much easier if the woman is convinced. However, while persuasion is ongoing, there is the tendency that the woman will lose a part of sexual arousal. In this case, the man would need to take the excitement back to a high level. Essentially then, he'd need to repeat the last three or four of the steps in chapter nine. Thoughtfully also, the man could repeat the step in which the woman showed utmost response as well. There wouldn't be the need to worry, where the woman had been aroused this far. To bring her back to an ideal level of sexual arousal wouldn't be difficult at all; feminine arousal doesn't wane as rapidly as that of men. Likewise, the use of romantic words during persuasion is enough to keep the woman at a good level of arousal. However, the moment she's well aroused again, then, it is time to move on to the core steps that will generate orgasms in multiple successions…. ***The Seven Crucial Steps***, the one below being the first.

…Using the left hand, gently pull up the woman's pubic area and simultaneously, open out the *labia majora*. To do this depiction, grasp the thumb and the index fingers in the shape of

letter 'V' but, in an inverted position. The three fingers remaining should be held in a slight upward fold. The hand is then placed at the upper end of the *labia majora*; the thumb and the index fingers, in inverted position, would be held together at their tips. Then, with the remaining three fingers in a slight upward fold, gently pull the woman's pubic flesh upwards. Thereafter, the thumb and the index fingers (slightly pushed into the *labia majora* at about mid-way) would be opened wide to gape the *labia majora*.

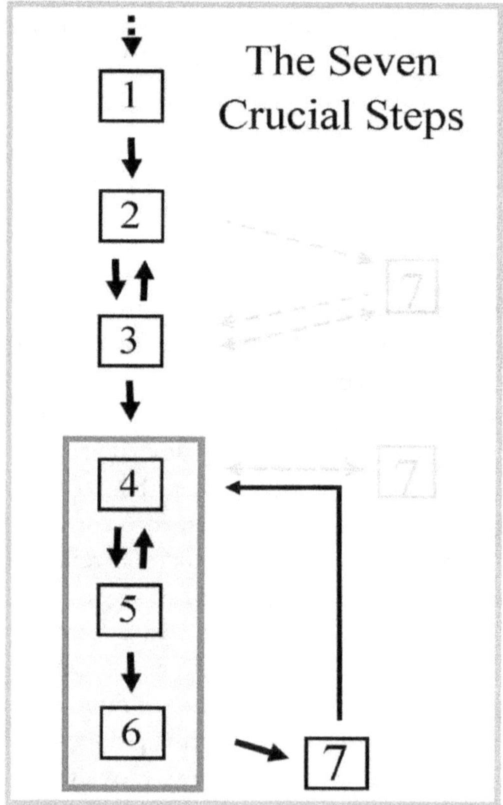

This action is a three-directional outward pull of the vulva using only the left hand. It's an act that'll expose the clitoris. Even if it's not seen, it's only not a large protrusion but there, and with this special way to pull, it'll be exposed. Notable here is that this special way of opening the vulva would be used in each of the subsequent step.

> *...Using the* right hand, raise the penis and touch the orifice of the vaginal passage, to take vaginal fluid with the penile tip. Spread it over the entire surface of the *labia majora* and up to the clitoris, to moisten the whole area within the vulva. It is important that smearing of fluid must occur on a regular basis, it is an aspect that cannot be stressed enough. Then, from its upper view, hold the penis in a scissors grip. To carry out this grip, hold the index and the middle fingers in an inverted letter "V" position.... These two fingers are then used to hold the penis, at about the middle of the penal span. Then, using the underneath of the penal cap, the penis is used to grind the clitoral area left and right ways. This horizontal grinding motion will be used to tickle the clitoris for as long as the man wishes.

> *...Clamp the penis* with the thumb on the upper side and on the underneath, with the index and the third fingers. In this position, it will be easier to carry out this step. Do not forget to take feminine fluid and smear as usual; of course, let it get to the clitoris as well. Using the underneath of the penile cap, *slowly tap on the clitoral region.* Ensure that this vertical oscillation is at a regular rate. Tap at a frequency of two to three times per second. Keep this action for as long as possible.

Steps two and three should be repeated back and forth, to avoid monotony and to prolong sensual pleasure for the woman. Additionally, there might be the need to chat romantically anywhere within these two steps!

> *...Go back to gentle* grinding motion, using the underneath of the penal cap, as it is in step two above. Repeatedly, take fluid as usual to lubricate the surface of the *labia majora.* Then, continue to grind on the clitoral region. At this time however, *gradually increase the speed of the action.* Tickle at a fast rate until more reaction from the woman is observable. De-

spite the high speed, this action should be sustained for as long as possible.

The woman's response would be easily evident; it might include the use of sounds and words to show that sensual excitement is in progress. Equally important at this point, is what the man is saying and his choice of words. Also, it is noticeable that with increased grinding speed, greater excitement would be created for the woman. If this is the first time of getting this far, the woman might want to back off for obvious reasons. Then, there might be the need to talk again! Once it is observable that the woman is willing to *play in the game*, then, the man should move on to the next step.

> **…*Similarly, go back to tapping*** in the same way as it is in the third step above. Simply move right from the quick grinding motion in the preceding step, into a slow tapping mode, in exactly the way it is in step three. Tap directly on the clitoral region and… at the same two to three taps per second. Now, in the same way as it is in step four, gradually ***increase*** the tapping speed until further reaction is noticeable.

How to elongate a sexual session? We'll get to that in a jiffy! In the meantime, steps four and five could also be repeated back and forth a couple of times, to drive sexual delight for the woman, a little further to higher levels. Within steps four and five, the man should try to reach a good speed. When the working speed increases beyond a particular level, the man would be in total control of the situation. Entirely, the woman would have succumbed to sexual pleasure. Events that'll unfold will dictate the rate at which to tap. Moreover, such events will guide on the power behind each tap and when to raise this power. The man would only need to be sure that the patter is directly on the clitoral area and at a steady speed. Consistently, he should lubricate the clitoral area. Similarly, he should be mindful of how steps two and three will end in steps four and five. Moreover, he should be aware that actions in steps four and five require the man to personalize his working speed to match up to the woman's response.

It would be observable that tapping is more effective on an average woman. So, the man should learn to be more skillful with the vertical than the horizontal movements. These vertical movements should be sufficiently used to realize desired results. Therefore, the man could stay relatively longer on the fifth step above to produce much delight for the woman. However, whether it is a pat with the hand or a tap with the penis, the woman could guide on the rate and power at which to strike, particularly, at the beginning. In this way, the man will learn more quickly, and he'll be able to accomplish more within a much shorter period of time. He'd have identified his woman's preference. Basically, the man should be gentle and with enormous self-confidence in all of these situations.

> ***...Essentially, the ongoing action of tapping*** at a high speed already attained in the preceding step five is made to spill over into this step. When the woman is about to achieve orgasm, a few highly noticeable reactions will serve as indicators. At this time, it is better **not** to lose the momentum already attained by attempting to smear feminine fluid. ***When properly done, this is the step that'll guide a woman into orgasm and as such, it must not be interrupted.*** Once the orgasmic indicator is noticed, instantly, the man should yet again, grow his speed. Likewise, he should quickly slip from tapping to not just tickling the clitoral region but to move at a speed that'll virtually be flicking the tip of the penis, at the highest rate conceivable. In addition, the man should guide his penis such that while *oscillating at this high speed, the tip of his penis will sprint back and forth across the clitoris, labia minora, and the urethral orifice and up to the vaginal opening.* This rapid oscillation should be sustained long enough, until the woman goes into and is done with the orgasm.

Steps four, five and six above are ***the three central steps***. In order to provide exceptional orgasms in multiple series to the woman, the man should bring his woman up to *the three central steps* above and thereafter, follow it in the form of a cycle, using the step below as the link. So, once the woman is through with an orgasm, instantly the man should move on to the step below. This is the step that'll turn the process into a cycle. Thus, the man will be able to take his woman through several orgasms. Repeatedly, he'd connect onto step four from seven, to go through the cycle again and again.

> ***...Hold the penis from above and at*** about the middle of its length in a scissors' grip, by using the index and the third

finger. These two fingers should be positioned on the left and on the right side of the penis, to form an inverted letter 'V' over it. To begin with, take more fluid to the clitoris as usual. With the scissors' grip, place the penis on the clitoris and then, move it in a slow grinding horizontal motion. This should be in a way that the underneath of the penile cap would brush back and forth on the clitoral region, as the penis is made to dash left and right ways.

The step above is the last of **the seven crucial steps**. Note that once the process that'll give multiple orgasms starts with step one of the seven crucial steps, it'll culminate in step six. This would produce an orgasm for the woman. More or less, step seven is a combination of slow steps one, two and three. The three central steps (four, five and six) only entail personalizing the rate at which to *work,* to measure up to the woman's response.

Chapter 12

Pleasantness

"…Love your wives, and be not bitter against them."
Colossians 3:19 (KJV)

Due to the attendant ease, when the three central steps in chapter eleven are repeated in a cycle, enormous sexual delight would be aroused in the woman. Of course, each cycle should culminate in orgasm. In the meantime, the three central steps are significant in two ways:

First: An agreeable ease with which the man could work is an indication that the use of the penile tip will *not* only replace cunnilingus… it will do so **with super-efficient stimulation, enormous speed and power** that the tongue can never cope with. This may be called, "**Penilingus**."

Second: Easily, tapping with the penile cap could replace a number of sex tools often turned down by women. It is a clever way of transforming the penis into a priceless tool. Precisely, *the biological tool every woman is craving for… is here*, being creatively utilized. This sexual approach has an unbelievable potential to energize feminine sexual excitement far beyond the imagination of either partner.

Similarly, the last step should also be done slowly at the beginning as observable response from the woman would be used to decide on when to raise the speed. All through this last step, romantic expressions by the man will also be suitable. Within step seven, it is likely that the amount of pressure while rubbing... is fairly immaterial. Basically, what is important is precisely... how to identify when to switch back to... *and then, go through* the three central steps all over again. Where a woman has just achieved an orgasm, step seven above should then be applied. In such a situation, the woman would easily be kept aroused. Visibly, in a short time, her sexual arousal will move up to a high level... again. This buildup of arousal would be observable in her response. While the man is offering the respite action of step seven, as soon as the woman's body response further becomes obvious, this would be the moment to start increasing the speed of the horizontal grinding motion. Soon afterwards, the man should move on to step four, and repeat the three central steps. ***Hence, taking the woman from steps one through six would lead to an orgasm for her. Afterward, each time she's made to go through the last four cyclic steps, she'd obtain an additional sequential orgasm.***

Thus, the last step... (step seven) is of **importance** in three ways:

> *First:* It adapts the three central steps into a cycle, by coupling itself in-between steps four and six.

> *Second:* The man is able to avert monotony in his action. This is when the step is slotted between steps two and three or used within step four. It will create variation in style.

> *Third:* It preserves the woman's arousal at a good level whenever there's the need to dialogue, relax or slow down for whatever reason.

Very significant is the man's left leg that is placed on the floor. Precisely, this should be used to do two things:

> **First...** To Adjust the Man's Body Position
> This will ease muscular cramp that'll discomfort due to being in an inconvenient sitting position.

Second... To Vary Tapping Points
When tapping spots are made to slightly vary, it'll further help to reduce monotony and at the same time, improve on the sexual excitement that could be created for the woman.

Deliberately, the low level of muscular ache the man will experience, in his awkward sitting position, is what he'll use to divert his own attention. Observably, the muscular ache wouldn't be much... however, if the man should hold on for a while, it'll multiply and produce diversion ample enough to distract his mind. The man will need to hold on to this pain for a moment before altering his position. Essentially, the intention is to give higher cognizance to the pain over sexual delight. In this way, he'd be able to play down on absorbing the entire reciprocal sexual delight his wife could potentially create for him. With a steady focus on this minor ache, the man should have a better grip on his sexual response. Hence, he may possibly *hold on* much longer than usual, to span the duration that's required by the woman to bring about a series of orgasms in successions. Hence, this is a prime strategy by which a woman could be made to savor the highly desired longer duration of sexual pleasure. Indeed, this would be a free and harmless approach by which a man could elongate a sexual session for as long as his partner wishes; it is a vital *tool* and... perpetually in the hands of the man.

Largely, for most women to achieve an orgasm, the seven crucial steps above will suffice. Thereafter, for orgasms to occur in multiple successions, repetition would have to be done as stated above. Thus, the man should **carry out the seven crucial steps until the woman has attained an orgasm**. Thereafter, he should **repeat the last four steps, three more times.** At this time, the woman would have had a total of four orgasms. However, the man shouldn't mention this yet. Meanwhile, the four orgasms should be taken as one **Ultimate Step**.

By whatever way, if the woman should demand a stop for the on-going sexual activities, before her fourth orgasm, the man would need to be observant. Such an action, once more, could be an effort to stop him from gaining insight into feminine deep sexuality. Thus, an assessment of the man's objectives may well incite this action, **to stop him from widening his misunderstanding of feminine deep sexuality.** Therefore, the man would need to quickly use persuasion, reinforced by honesty; …the same approach stated earlier. The moment attraction is seen once more in the woman, the man should move on to the next step. As earlier stated, the man should know that an average woman may not unveil her deep sexuality, except when she's thoroughly convinced that the man is entirely aware of benefits that could be derived. Moreover, she might not succumb until the man is able to prove sincerity in his pursuit.

Caringly then, the man should slow down if the woman is persistent. However, due to the reason identified above, it should at least, be after the third or the fourth orgasm. In the meantime, using romantic words, the man should mention the intent to offer, right on a silver platter, a total of ten orgasms for her delight. Tell her to relax and pleasantly, to absorb each one. In addition, it would be beautiful if the man could expose how much delightful he was while making her accomplish orgasms. Nevertheless, while chatting, do not completely *stop*, only slow down and… go into step seven. In the interim, repeatedly smear the feminine fluid, covering the whole area within the *labia majora*. On the other hand, if she's interested in the *game*, all the same, the man should slow down at the end of the fourth orgasm; then, he should move on to the magical step seven, as already described above. The next step would be to go from step seven back to step four and repeat the process for obtaining four orgasms described in the paragraph before the last. At any rate, the moment this process becomes successful with a couple, there'll be a better flow at subsequent attempts.

An observable effect within the seventh step is that it provides an opening to give a moment of respite to the woman. The woman's body reaction in the step is though very gentle, but it's the evidence that elation is ongoing. Anyhow, as soon as noticeable reaction becomes lively, it is a sign that the woman is relishing the stimulation. Then, it is time for a gradual increase in speed. When this speed is high enough, sustain it for a while and then, move on to step four. At that point, the man should perform the actions identified in the three central steps, as described above. Also, he should go over the cycle four times, to complete one other ultimate step. At the end of this, the woman would've had additional series of four orgasms. As soon as this is over, the man should stay within step seven as usual, for a chat.

Curiously, if the three central steps in the cyclic form are repeated in four quick successions, four orgasms would be obtained for the woman. For simplicity reasons, the whole process of getting four orgasms for a woman will be bundled into one *Ultimate Step*. The ultimate step is a remarkable one that could be repeated as many times as preferred by the couple. In the meantime, the size of the ultimate step could be kept at either three or four orgasms due to personal preference. Hence, four of such ultimate steps could make the woman achieve between twelve and up to sixteen multiple orgasms, while the man is still very fresh and devoid of tiredness. In this way, the woman could be made to reach as many orgasms as her body dictates. Clearly, any woman that is brought up to this erotic level could be sexually satiated. Therefore, ***the ultimate step should be repeated as preferred,*** *depending on couple's outlook. During each repetition, the man should try to get four orgasms for the woman.* Certainly, a display of romantic boldness via words, the expression of fondness for the entire procedure, and similar thoughts could intensify the woman's curiosity and support for the process.

At the end of three ultimate steps, this is the time to ask the woman for the number of orgasms she must have had so far. It is noteworthy that in quick successions, to have taken the woman through three ultimate steps, she'd have been made to achieve not less than nine and as much as twelve orgasms. For clear reasons then, she would have either lost count or, she wouldn't be bothered anymore about counting. Without losing a second, the man should move on to step seven normally…. As for the update, he should as lovingly as possible, inform the woman that it could be five or six orgasms. Once the fourth ultimate step is over, the man should move on to step seven as usual…. While he's within the seventh step, he could offer the words… nine or ten orgasms. By this time, it is certain that the woman would have achieved between twelve and up to sixteen orgasms. Some loving words would be magical here too, simply couple them with equally magical step seven. While the seventh step is ongoing, the man should offer to give one more orgasm. He could tag it using any suitable name… ***a special offer to round off the day.*** Of course, his intention wouldn't be anything different from helping his woman to take one more ultimate step. In no time, the man will realize and amazingly too, that a woman is a special creation; she could take more…! As usual, move from the seventh step and lovingly, go over the three central steps to carry out a cycle. Thereafter, go over these cyclic steps three more times, to carry out one more ultimate step. Consequently, a woman could have had a total of between fifteen and twenty orgasms.

Conspicuously, within the preceding paragraph, incorrect numbers were to be cited by the man for his woman. This situation is not about dishonesty. The intention rather, is to create a brilliantly pleasant experience for the woman. It is an attempt to deploy service providers' thinking that says, "*...Under promise, but over deliver.*" Within the extent of diverse marital obligations, it is predictably clear that the sexual technique described in this book is fair enough. It is what any man could carry out and... devoid of deceit. Thus, subsequent trials should be open for either partner to make relevant contributions at every stage.

To conclude the sexual session, the man will have to place himself in a way that a change in body positioning will be convenient, as soon as it is necessary. He could prop up his body using the left foot, on the floor, and his right knee, on the bed. At that point, his buttocks would be lifted up a little off the bed, with the right leg folded backwards at the knee. *After the last* feminine orgasm, the man should change his body positioning entirely, to have primary sensual contact, without losing a moment. With just a little more attention from the man, the woman may achieve an additional orgasm, at the same time with that of the man. If not, she'd not mind, having achieved between fifteen and twenty multiple orgasms in a quick series. Later on, the man may want to evaluate his action and its effect on the woman. Then, he should try to stay awake a little longer. Almost certainly, there would be a difference in both the woman's attitude and actions, as opposed to the usual trend. Assuredly, this would be the beginning; if honest intentions are sustained by the man, the woman will come out of sexual passivity. Then...!

Chapter 13

Additional Tip

"Not as though I had already attained... but I follow after...."
Philippians 3:12 (KJV)

Sexual intercourse in men is presumed as being dependent on at least two ideas; a jumbo-sized tool and, the power behind thrust action. Totally, these two opinions are erroneous. However, the most unfortunate issue is that it could be really difficult to make an average man accept any other opinion.

How relevant is an extra-large tool? When the situation is sexual, it is a special one. It is where women in particular, recurrently consider **efficient use of the masculine tool** as being more important than its size. **Often, a plus size penis is viewed as a doubtful gift from a man, by an average woman.** As a matter of fact, a woman would go for a smaller piece that could be capably deployed. In addition, and surprisingly too, she'll do it **whenever and wherever** the opportunity is offered.

"Every man has his price...." In the same way, every **man** will seize what is personally considered as the right opportunity. In other words, it is a big wonder to observe some men believe that their spouses wouldn't indulge in infidelity. Essentially, the fact is the more conservative a woman is, believe it or not, the more stringent will be the settings she'll use to grab sexual opportunities. To keep infidelity out of a marriage, the man must know that the solution is not in looking for an extra-large tool. Also, he must understand what a woman considers as… utilization of the masculine tool in an efficient manner. ***If a plus sized penis will not deliver the idea laid out in this book, such a tool is absolutely useless to any woman.***

How crucial is the focus on thrust action? In sexual awareness, an average man is yet to understand that thrust action should not necessarily be similar to the forceful action of a locomotive engine. This is not an attempt to nullify prods during sexual sessions, but to reveal an essential purpose for its use. ***Thrusts… should be used to create the space for a particular action.*** The moment an attempt is being made by the man to create room for this action, the woman will understand that she's got a man who knows what to do. ***Watch out, at that moment, she'll offer ample room for him to carry out an efficient maneuver!***

Of course, there's an action that is very essential, but… it'll come in a moment. Whenever sexual sessions will not be as detailed as earlier described, the man could still be thorough. As the more dynamic partner, a man's major focus is to penetrate and immediately start a thrust action. Time and again, this'll happen within the shortest possible time. However, important steps may include the following:

> ***…Allow the woman*** to contribute to foreplay, she's got a few exciting actions to offer. First, this will be easier if the woman has been effectively pulled out of sexual passivity. Also, this is a step that'll help grow a man's sexual response; ***it'll grant him the ability to last for a couple of essential seconds more, during the primary act.***

> ***…Before the start*** of the primary act, ensure that ***entry*** will be smooth, and easy.

> ***…Immediately after the*** step above, never rush into the next step below; wait for a while ***within….*** This action has a further exciting effect on the woman. If properly done, she wouldn't be able to conceal the delight in the step that'll follow.

> ***…To start the*** first cycle of thrust, the man should simultaneously ***press-up and pull upwards.*** This action should be

sudden and without any cue to the woman. From then on, repeated thrusts could follow.

*...**The third and** the fourth steps above could be done once or twice, to grow feminine arousal and delight. Thereafter, this should lead to the big one in the next step below.

*...**Once movement starts**, the man should be mindful that **thrust action** shouldn't be the only means for creating sexual pleasure for the woman. Rather, it should be used to create room for the necessary action described below. However, action gaps in any of the steps could be filled with **appropriate** romantic words.

Really, whatsoever purpose one might have for thrust action should be secondary. Certainly, there is an action that's very essential, and **here it is...**

*...**To make sure that each thrust will end in a tap on the woman's clitoral area, using the man's pubic region.**

This essential action has four pertinent steps...:

...Tapping should be done using the lower part of the man's pubic region; the part directly above the penile base.

...The man should make sure that tapping is firm enough to be felt right on the clitoris.

At this point, the man should attempt to deliver tapping action with much gentleness and... at a regular speed. With a deft touch, tapping would be accompanied by a fairly loud patter sound. In the meantime, adulthood would teach that in whatever way before then, the patter sound should be prevented from being heard outside the bedroom.

For clear reasons, no woman will allow any man with a penile length that's longer than her birth canal, to carry out the erotic action stated here. As a result, men should disregard cravings for extra length. As for penile girth, it is a medical expert and the woman concerned that can tell. Nevertheless, if penile girth is to become an issue, the man should understand that within a wide range… the woman is biologically gifted with an expedient solution. This feminine control makes a great deal of relief available for an incredibly large proportion of men. On the other hand, help could be obtained from a medical center. With relief from either of these two sources, the man's attention and emphases should be on the purpose for this guide book.

> *…Gradually, the rate of patter should be increased and, this should be taken up to a high yet regular speed.* On speed handling, see the *Seven Crucial Steps in the preceding chapter.*

> *…When the time is right, the high speed should be kept steady and… sustained through feminine crucial moments.*

> *While taking the four related steps above, the man must* **pair his prod action and recurrent tapping** *on the woman's clitoral region using his own pubic region, into two concurrent actions. Equally notable is the fact that this double action has nothing to do with a power-backed action which could collapse his bedroom structure.*

Using these simultaneous actions, it is important to take note of the following facts:

> …For women, this is an action that generates greater delight from two sensual sources and at the same time. However, there must be no hasty push, it should be made gradual.

> …The potential effect obtainable from this action is what the woman is aiming at, each and every time she's the *active* partner.

> …From this outlook, it could be observed that men's sexual act isn't about a large penis. In this situation, it is noticeable that penile reach is almost… if not completely irrelevant!

> …Thrust? This is an action that is misunderstood by men the world over; it is wrongly used as a replica of a power-piling machine.

…Finally, described above is a situation in which the man's work will be similar to that of the remote-control device for a bulldozer, and not the Earthmover equipment itself.

There's no doubt the entire procedure, as described within chapters nine to twelve, is elaborate and workable mostly on special days. In this chapter, the portion described above is quite similar to what could be presently observed in most bedrooms. The slight difference is in the depth of coital penetration which of course, has a purpose. Certainly, it is pertinent to note that the purpose for the depth of penetration is why an average woman is asking for such an action; she wants to simultaneously couple pleasures from two sources. This is the idea most men have misinterpreted for a locomotive action! By now, an average man should know that this double action takes a woman to the peak of sexual arousal within a short period of time.

Sprinkled on quite a few pages of this book is… how to bring a woman out of sexual passivity. In this chapter, the importance is no less. The man has to be skillful well enough to deploy these two actions at the same time. Then, the woman could be pulled naturally… to help her man; she'll be motivated to give a support. In addition, she'll be willing to assume an all-exposing position required; she'd have been aroused well enough to consider certain actions as necessary.

To have a better process flow, it is proper to divide this chapter into two halves, the portion above being the second. The reason for this reverse order will show up just before the end of the chapter. For now, here comes the first half.

As stated above, the entire process in chapters nine to twelve guarantees absolute satisfaction for either partner. In the meantime, when peculiar demand by other life activities – work, children, social interactions and more are considered, there'd be the need for a quick-fix procedure! Such a procedure will be appropriate and easy to apply by virtually every couple.

Now, the crucial procedure is about to show up! …A technique that'll be prompt enough to compress the entire long process into a short yet comprehensive action…? Then, what's coming up will be the big… BANG! This action will help the man to focus on giving two to five successive orgasms to a woman, on a regular basis - regardless of personal rate of sexual occurrence and without an iota of tiredness. Of course, this hurried technique could be used long enough to ensure much more than ten multiple orgasms for the woman. Oh yeah, any man who just read the last line could pinch himself… it isn't a dream. Additionally, the story behind the process isn't much, simply deepen the required attention as much as possible…; remember, the author not being a native speaker of the English language will continue to face perceptible grammar challenges.

A start off from unpleasant scenarios will clarify the extent to which this method-compression could be relevant and useful. A typical instance is where the woman is partially indifferent to sexual overtures from her man. Within her mind, "…it's going 'o be game as usual." To worsen this scenario is the commonly observed scanty foreplay from most men. A second case is when she comes home tired and heavy…. Meanwhile, the man held on to sensual imaginations fired up during the day by unintentional but vivid imageries. As such, he's slyly and relentlessly offering slimy gel in a turgid capsule as a potent elixir for the woman's tiredness. In this case, the effect of commonly observed micro prelude by men, which hitherto was insufficient, will be coupled with a shallow level of cooperation from the woman, to worsen feminine response. An added example is when the woman isn't expecting sexual intercourse at all.

In these or similar circumstances, the woman may have little or no arousal. As a result, she could be bruised or at best… have tickling feeling when touched. Once this difficulty is predictable, the first step is to have whatever could serve as lubricant handy. The use of saliva might seem offensive to some people. Besides, it's an avoidable avenue for transferring bacteria from the mouth to the vagina. However, a perfect and cost-effective alternative recommended by the author of this book, is the use of a few drops of clean table water; it is remarkable. The quick-fix method is code-named… ***"Multiple Sashays."*** In a while, this name will be explained. In this method, the use of penilingus – as described in the opening paragraph of chapter twelve - is flexibly easy, extensive and requires little or no exertion in the least. The couple's body-position is as shown in figure three; it's a head-on position regularly preferred by women.

> ***…The*** man will kneel down on the bed. He'll move so as to have the woman's buttocks in-between his knees, keeping her legs extended as much as it's convenient… beyond his body.

This movement is ***the first glide***; it's the start-off glide. This being an attempt to bring out a reason for the name… *multiple sashays.*

*…**Place*** the penile tip at the vaginal orifice; …no penetration whatsoever. Add a couple of drops of sparkling table water, letting it drip from labia minora down to the position of the penis. As in the case of a right-hand user, the man will shape the fingers on his left hand in the inverted letter "V" position. This action is as described in chapter eleven; it is repeated below for convenience…

"…Using the left hand, gently pull up the woman's pubic area and simultaneously, open out the labia majora. To do this depiction, grasp the thumb and the index fingers in the shape of letter 'V' but, in an inverted position. The three fingers remaining should be held in a slight upward fold. The hand is then placed at the upper end of the labia majora; the thumb and the index fingers, in inverted position, would be held together at their tips. Then, with the remaining three fingers in a slight upward fold, gently pull the woman's pubic flesh upwards. Thereafter, the thumb and the index fingers (slightly pushed into the labia majora at about mid-way) would be opened wide to gape the labia majora."

Figure Three

> ***…Thereafter,*** go straight on to penilingus. Brush the tip of the penis in a rapid up and down moves… across the vulva. Keep darting from the labia minora, over the clitoris, down to the vaginal orifice and back. Start off in a playful style. Remember, the position showing in figure three above is quite easy and convenient. So, start slowly and gradually… grow the speed.

The fact that the most appropriate and preferred tool is being used, she'll not experience any discomfort! The moment she savors pleasure from this action, her first response could be to ask for a full penetration; she either wants more or she wants to get it done with. With the most suitable tool, non-offensive lubricant, zero discomfort, and a tenacious work on her clit, simply ask her to take a little more of the pleasure. Continue and in a short while, pleasure from her clit will take over, to arouse her fascination. With the biological tool still in use, her next reaction will be to slightly raise her legs. She'll fold up her knees towards her chest. This is ***the second glide***; it's the information glide. In the meantime, she's trying to offer a couple of supportive steps; …to create enough room that'll aid the man's action; and… to further expose her clitoris for greater effect. ***Within these supportive steps lies the enclave wherein an average man has that absolute control with which to take his spouse to sexual satisfaction that's hitherto a mirage.***
With the woman's knees folded towards her chest region, she'd have moved a little away from where the man could make a perfect contact. On his knees, the man should move closer, to maintain a firm contact. This body movement by the man is ***the third glide;*** it's the maintenance glide. Noteworthy is the fact that the second and the third glides are within the third step.

> ***…The*** next step is to grow the rate at which the man is darting, up and down, to a tremendously high level. Using his penile tip, he should rub on the woman's vulva in upward and downward strokes.

Although the action in the last step above is meant to occur in hastily repeated vertical movements, it comprises ***the fourth glide;***

it is the rattling glide. It's where the method itself got the name… multiple! Once this last step has been reached, the man will maintain the high darting speed until his woman achieves an orgasm. Basically, the entire procedure within multiple sashays is an expansion of a small portion at about the end of the sixth step in chapter eleven. Using multiple sashays, a clear observation will be that the time required by an average woman to reach an orgasm is not as long as wrongly presumed. Practically, this last step could be repeated over and over again, to ensure as many multiple orgasms as preferred by the woman concerned. Each repetition will provide an orgasm for the woman without the smallest fragment of tiredness on the man. Creatively, the step could be sustained long enough to provide a number of orgasms in a nonstop series for a woman. This action will make it possible for anyone to verify the fact by Wikipedia, detailed in chapter ten, that women have no refractory period.

> *…To* close the sexual session, the man should revert to the procedure outlined in the upper half of this chapter. Most likely, he'd be able to add one more orgasm to those previously attained by his woman. This is that crucial moment the man will take his own orgasm. If carefully done, an added orgasm for the woman will coincide with that of the man.

Significantly, taking this lower half of this chapter before the upper half has an obvious reason in favor of the masculine nature. Almost certainly, the man will be satiated after just one orgasm, unlike the woman. Every man should understand that during sexual intercourse, an average woman will need to reach between two and five orgasms in multiple successions; the closer to five… the better. Then, feminine sexual satisfaction will show up naturally. Below is an excerpt towards the end of chapter five of… "The Manly Man…"

> *"…Be mindful of the fact that a woman does not have a refractory period. This is why some men alleged that women are sexually insatiable. …This is entirely a wrong notion…; She'll have to use her mind in whichever of two ways…. The first is… when the woman is sexually satisfied…. The second, though boringly exasperating… is a part of virtually every woman…!"*

From Adam to Eve…

To conclude, the quick-fix method is quite easy. The man will make use of muscles from his arm rather than within his tongue. As a result, he'll be able to grow his working speed up to a rattling level. The capability of the muscles involved is much more than what the muscles in his tongue could ever cope with. Also, within this method, every communication tactic possible, including the few stated within chapters eleven and twelve could be deployed by the man. This is a technique an average woman will find amenable. With this sexual technique, the man should look out for an offer of appreciation, sexual excitement and more… on a silver platter. In the last chapter, there's more on what the man should expect.

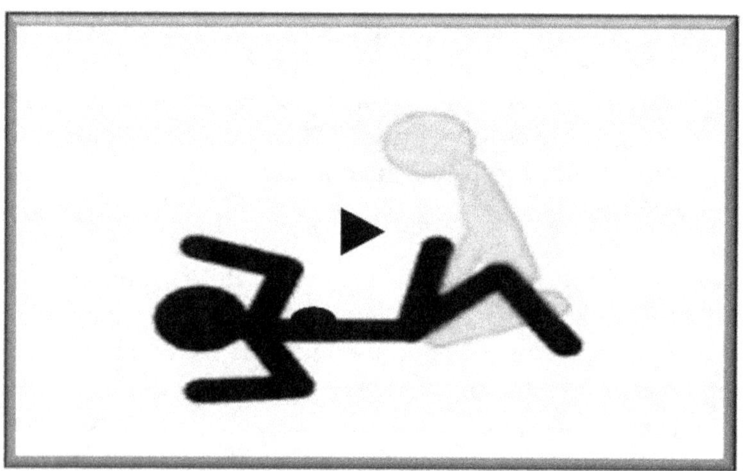

(To see a video-like representation of the image, click on the figure).
Video clip is available in eBook format only.

Chapter 14

Give It to Her

"Drink waters out of thine own cistern, and running waters out of thine own well."

Proverbs 5:15 (KJV)

Unquestionably, it is as easy as detailed here. Research experts have established that when they achieve orgasm, women would wait a couple of seconds at the peak level of arousal. Likewise, it's been shown that when they eventually start to come out of arousal, they will do so also slowly. Logically, when these two ideas are tied to the fact that women do not go through refractory period, then, there is a strong point in favor of multiple orgasms. Equally, it is noticeable that the first orgasm requires a longer time than subsequent ones. So, first off, the man must take his time to prolong foreplay. Next, is to make use of a suitable method that could get the woman to the peak level of arousal. Then, the first orgasm should occur. At that point, if this means is sustained for a longer time beyond the first orgasm, thereafter, orgasms in multiple series should occur. Of course, successive orgasms after the first one would be easily realized and really, occurring at times that are not too far apart.

Each time the man changed from rapid tapping over to horizontal tickling and rubbing, the woman became calm. Nevertheless, the moment vertical tapping resumed, her reaction was almost immediate; precisely, she started off from where the intensity of stimulation was lowered, regardless of a few seconds that had elapsed. The simple explanation one could provide for this is that the woman must have waited for a while at the peak level of arousal. Probably, she'd just started her slow downward glide, when the right touch brought back sensual excitement.

An important consideration is if this method will be used at a time not far away from feminine orgasm, when it was necessary to chat. The man would have slowed down, into horizontal tickling and rubbing coupled with the use of romantic words. Essentially, these actions are part of what would keep the woman at the peak level of arousal. Religiously using the mode up to the end would bring about feminine orgasms in multiple series. Here then is a simple way to observe the amazing aspect of feminine sexuality, where sexual arousal does not instantaneously wane after the incidence of orgasm. So, it is a sexual method that men could make use of to ensure multiple orgasms for women. Feminine arousal that wanes pretty slowly is a remarkable issue. Its full effect will be more profound when a woman is not made to achieve a pleasing sexual climax. In a woman, the lack of regular orgasm is a sad event that must be avoided; it is a leading cause of devastation on women's emotion.

In contrast, it is uncommon for a man to attain the first orgasm and remain at the topmost level of arousal. As a result, it is usually rare afterwards for a man to continue to perform; perhaps, his penis might no longer be sufficiently turgid. Although it's not impossible to find men who could go up to the second and probably the third orgasm without a stoppage period, but only in rare cases do this occur. For men, it is likely that orgasms beyond the first one, would take more time and exertion. Commonly, an average man would be satiated at the end of a sexual session delineated for men by masculine orgasm. To attain the second and perhaps more orgasms, most men would likely be required to enhance their libido. (***Please, this book does not approve sexuality enhancement. For anyone who wants to do so, a stern advice is for such individual to first off, get the opinion of a medical doctor. To practice the method herein described, the use of products in whatever form to boost men's sexuality is entirely not necessary***).

Undoubtedly, when the approach in this book is applied, it would be discovered that an immediate attempt at a second orgasm by men may be needless. Apparently, the intention of most men, when they try to achieve a second orgasm, is commonly not inspired by personal favor but to sexually satisfy their spouse. Additionally, even with a push for the second or more sexual sessions, perhaps, an average man would only be able to make his woman achieve only a couple of orgasms. In such a case, the woman would, once in a while, yearn for more as long as her sexual desire is yet to be satiated. As said in the preceding chapter, the woman's desire could be satiated slightly above 20% but far below 30%. Meanwhile, with the method described in this book, the woman's sexual desire would not only be satisfied but repeatedly as often as the woman desires and without an iota of fatigue for the man.

Earlier on, it might be difficult…; however, this is where an agreement could be reached on the fact that women are blessed more than men in sexuality. Although this is a personal submission, it is from a personal observation of over twenty years. An analogy to describe the situation, which may not be the best, is that while men are in search of how to produce cold water, women already are expert ice makers. Simply, this is to describe a wide gap that's apparently visible between men and women in terms of sexual response. The effect of this gap is more noticeable in men who have not acquired sufficient information about feminine sexuality. Therefore, in all aspects, women have superior and desirable sexual capabilities than an average man. As a result, women could exhibit sexual exuberance much more than an average man but would safely tuck it away, beneath a heavy cloud of pretense that is managed by instinct, to dissuade the attention of her skeptical mate from a misconception.

There's been growth in the level of sexuality awareness in the last couple of decades and this has revealed much, particularly about women. This is why men are desperate to improve on their sexual response; a large number of men are seeking how to perform a little better. Precisely, this is why research work has and will continue to hurl out different forms of products particularly, in an effort to enhance sexual dexterity in men. Furthermore, it is the reason for evolving a sexual method like oral sex. By the use of Cunnilingus, the man has the conviction that he is sexually efficient a little more. Though, in recent times, the drawback is the scary health risk that has been linked to it. Surely, with the mode detailed in this book, as said earlier, the spread of Sexually Transmittable Diseases is also possible. However, the danger could well be reduced in the same way as it is commonly done. Meanwhile, using the approach in this book, men's sexual response would immensely be superior to whatever extent any other *unaided* method could possibly proffer.

After a humble reflection, one could conclude that sexual starvation should be viewed as not just a dearth of sexual intercourse. It could be said to include situations where a woman is yet to reach at least an orgasm, and have had to endure associated mental stress, despite the occurrence of sexual sessions at preferred frequencies with her spouse. Possibly, this situation could be worse on a woman when medical fears are absent in her man. Also, in the 1970s, Helen Singer Kaplan admitted that emotions of anxiety, safety and failure of communication could impede one's sexual desire and hence orgasm. This is factual and could affect both male and female in similar situations. Hence, under favorable social conditions, any woman that's not sexually satiated should be expected to suffer emotional devastation as well. As such, when there are concerns – medical or psychological, visits should be made to lawful professionals for resolutions.

Meanwhile in the 1980s, Rosemary Basson proposed that orgasm is just one point in the orgasmic cycle rather than being the peak of sexual experience. Thus, she concluded that, "People could feel sexually satisfied at any stage." This suggestion would totally eliminate the significance of orgasmic climax as a beneficial and a highly desirable aspect of sexual intercourse. Merely reading this could set off a hopeless feeling of withdrawal for an average man; men constantly savor the pleasure of orgasm and can tell better. As a result, no man would accept to have an inconclusive sexual activity. It'll be worse to deny a man of orgasm just when he's approaching one. A denial will be unacceptable when his mind and body has been set in sexual motion that should culminate in orgasm. Of course, no man will consent to this, except he's been over-sexed lately. Even if he's been over-sexed, it is only when his effort is not yielding the desired result that he'd likely abandon his orgasmic hunt and notably, it's only for that moment. Apparently, Basson's idea sounds more like a conjecture meant to prove that orgasm is irrelevant in women. Absolutely, it supports women's typical bogus defense that, "*Orgasm isn't a necessity for women…*" as stated in chapters one and nine. This is a planned attempt to hide feminine profound sexuality that was incorrectly thought to require an extremely grueling bed-top exercise from men. Even with outright disregard or absence for scientific facts, it will be wrong for anyone to nullify the import of orgasm in women. At this time, if one may query, ***isn't it an absolute fact that the woman didn't design her own body physiology?*** If this is true, then, why disagree with what is divine, pleasant, and rich and obviously, unalterable? Indeed, there must be a way round this outdated notion… it is here detailed in this book. Certainly, "We can do nothing against the truth, but for the truth…" 2nd Corinthians 13:8 (KJV).

As expected by every man, the climax at which every sexual activity comes to an end is orgasm. It's the point at which an individual gain hugely from sex. Repeatedly, it is where everyone would plan to reach. Obviously, this is a dictate by Biology, and women can do nothing but to conform as well. So, kindly let's add that Basson's idea stated earlier on, is not just obsolete but out of tune with physically observable actions, and the enormous amount of information already published by the scientific world. So, no woman, not a single person for whatever reason, should be allowed to go through a sexual session without an orgasm, especially when the purpose is to have one. For any woman who does not enjoy regular orgasmic joy, it will be nothing but insensitivity, neglect and probably, wickedness on the part of her man. Where a man is able to offer regular orgasmic experience for his spouse, there would be a decrease in irrational wandering around erotic fantasies. At a level beyond moderation, sensual fantasies triggered by lack of orgasmic joy and sexual satisfaction, could lead to a buildup of dangerous secrecy. Ultimately, this buildup could manifest as a true social *bomb*, which often would detonate… to smash a marriage.

Experts have proved that men fantasize daily about sex, or at least more often than women. Sheridan Simove, the author of an exciting book title, "What Every Man Thinks About Apart from Sex" (2011), after several years of careful personal observation, was able to imply (from the *contents* of his book) that men think totally about nothing apart from sex. For that reason, the antidote for a married man's unremitting sexual fantasy is orgasm, orgasm and orgasm. Certainly, this must be as and when desired, otherwise the man will nurture a means, and actually get one outside his home. Undeniably, this is an antidote that's also available to women. Anyhow, in this case, the man should be held responsible if the woman is not getting the antidote as she should. The reason is due to the fact that an average woman would, before any other means, seek sexual gratification first from her man.

From Adam to Eve…

The moment sexual intercourse has been completed by a man (an activity that will predictably climax in orgasm) sexual moods would be out of his thoughts. Easily, this would be noticeable when the man tries to do four or five orgasms within a space of an hour. For a man, the second and hence further orgasms will require extra effort to attain. In the extreme situation, an attempt by a man to naturally procure up to ten orgasms for himself, within a time limit of two consecutive hours honestly could be viewed as an unbearable task. The extent of *work* that'd be required would be highly grueling. Certainly, it would be enough to dissipate the physical strength of any man up to the point of having the sensation of illness, which might linger on for a couple of days. Moreover, such a mission if attempted could make a man sexually numb for up to twelve hours, if not more. The numbness could be so deep that the man may not, within a good period of time, pick on overt sexual signals from another woman. In addition, within the period of numbness, fantasizing about sex would equally be outside his considerations.

In the meantime, men should put themselves in women's shoes and, experiment using at least, ten sexual contacts. This should be done at couples' ordinary rate of sexual activities. The man should ensure that he does not reach orgasm on each occasion. Thereafter, he could visualize and draw conclusions on how women feel when made to experience a large number of sexual contacts, and are yet deprived of orgasms. Clearly, this is a test that'll explain the statement by a respectable, elderly American best-selling author, Naura Hayden that, "The commonest complaint from children, about mothers, is nagging and raising the voice at the least of provocation; an action depicting frustrated, angered and tense mothers, taking it out on their children." Of course, the source of frustration in these women is devastated emotions which could have been soothed by satisfying sex. Also, within the period of this humble personal observation, men should pay close attention to how attractive they consider every other woman they come across. This will shed light on the extent of hopelessness suffered by women due to lack of orgasmic pleasure. Furthermore, it'll show the degree of exposure to sexual infidelity that women in this situation have to manage, day in… day out.

In a normal sexual interaction, a single orgasm will often satisfy the man. However, what's worthy of note is that women, with an innate ability, could achieve ten or more orgasms in one sexual interaction. Since women have the ability to reach multiple orgasms with ease, most likely then, the effect of men's single orgasm will be equivalent to what could be gained by women in multiple orgasms. Then, give it to her…! It is feasible and could be done by anyone. In this book, it has been shown that ten or more successive orgasms for the woman could be offered in a way the man will not be tired at all. Thus, during regular sexual contacts, the man should help his woman to achieve a number of orgasms that'll depend on her preference. Afterwards, the big one could be reserved for special occasions. As such, when the intention is not to have the big one, the man could regularly make use of the position in figure three… at about the end of chapter thirteen.

Let's also add that when multiple orgasms are given to a woman, the man will get to know what his spouse may not have fully discovered about herself. The notion that women are good-looking is not an exaggeration. Right from the moment a woman succumbs to absolute sexual arousal and essentially, as she's made to go through orgasms, the man will understand that she's a beauty to behold. Within the orgasmic phase, the woman's beauty radiates vividly, and she is lovely to observe. Of course, this is the period when the woman would have lost the capacity to either conceal her feelings or show a cautious handling of her reactions. This would be an exceptional situation; it is when a man will make a discovery that'll be special… and personal too. At that point, the woman's expressions will show feminine sexuality that is candidly uncovered. This period is when a man will revel in sexual delight that'll nicely and repeatedly, lure him back to his woman. Ably, the occurrence that is luring the man back to sexual delight in his home could ultimately, reduce marital infidelity in his thinking. The man wouldn't have only offered sexual satisfaction to his woman… he would have incited his woman to respond unconsciously too. In other words, this elementary action the man will have to get going personally, has enormous potential to constantly generate endless mutual sexual excitement in… and for his marriage, to safeguard the same marriage.

Evidently, more studies would be required…. However, if a balanced experimentation could be set up, then, when the item producing stimulus is sustained for between two and ten minutes beyond the first orgasm, the gender with the ability to achieve more orgasms in quick successions would be identified. Accordingly, after comparing what is observable in behavioral pattern of men and women, conclusions on multiple orgasms can only be in favor of *the feminine gender.*

It is a known fact that after the first orgasm, the man's sexual enthusiasm will drop rapidly. To achieve another orgasm, he has to build his sexual desire from zero level up again. From men with the best of ability, this may require a couple of seconds. But, on the other side of the divide, this **recovery** could take days to achieve. Thus, in a man, every orgasm in reality is a discrete sexual event.

Hence, men's orgasms instantly after the first one would progressively be dull or difficult to procure particularly, in situations where pharmaceutical and/or nutritional aids, recognized to cut refractory period in individuals are absent. Plainly, it would naturally be intolerable for a man to attain ten orgasms in rapid, non-stop successions, within a space of an hour. On the other hand, for women to achieve ten orgasms or more in quick successions is a notion that's as easy as winking. Moreover, these series of feminine orgasms could be crowded into an incredibly short period of time. Amazingly, the whole process could be finalized in much less than one hour, if the factor that produced the first orgasm is properly sustained. Indeed, this orgasmic series is multiple orgasms. This display of multiple orgasms can thus be associated with women and obviously, not men. At any rate, while we wait for results from further research work, it would be safe to urge men to exploit this humble notion. Therefore, with the sexual method described in this book, a man could aim for the number of sexual rounds he could naturally cope with, and still give maximum sexual satisfaction to his spouse. This is the way it ought to be.

Via the method presented in this book, sexual features an average man would be able to accomplish might include the following:

> …Ability to sexually satiate his woman.
> At any time, a man could treat his spouse beyond her expected sexual outlook. The woman would be helped up to where she'd be sexually satiated. As such, the man could achieve one orgasm, then, go through his refractory period and without any anxiety; he'd have satisfied his woman's desire.
> …Perform devoid of fatigue.

Efficiently, men could perform bed-top exercise beyond feminine anticipation and without getting exhausted at all.
…Discover man's hidden ability.
Inborn in an average man is a massive capability with which he could balance a woman's enviable sexual response. It's a unique ability that men could exploit as repeatedly as preferred.
…Share sexual benefit with his woman.
The fact that the man could offer what is naturally scheduled for the woman's body, she's now able to partake in the benefit obtainable from sex.
…Reduce unnecessary issues.
Sexual satisfaction in the home is an all-important issue; capably, it will cut adverse health and social trepidations connected to natural sex.

It is noteworthy that any sexual mode that ensures sexual satisfaction for a woman would be an indispensable key with which to unlock a stress-free living for the woman and ultimately, for the man. The woman will be stress-free to help as her man's suitable companion. After this, she'll constantly be in the right frame of mind to exude feminine abilities. Entirely, she'll be able to use women's divinely endowed aptitude to…:

…Keep a peaceful home and,
…Get attracted to and love the man more deeply.

At this point, it is pertinent for every man to note that… when the intention is to create sensual satisfaction for the woman, the use of sexual heightening products meant to be swallowed by men are not only wrong, but raise multiple hazards. Agreed, a boost for the man will help extend his rigorous work… an action that might be used to create two to five series of feminine orgasms. Using such a booster with the intention of creating ten or more orgasms… it is clear that no woman will be willing to bear the risk, even when an average could take much more than twelve orgasms in succession without exhaustion. Additionally, the attendant labor could end the life of an average man! In the meantime, the right approach will make the entire process absolutely effortless.

From Adam to Eve…

Chapter 15

Here We Are

"When wisdom entereth into thine heart...;
Discretion shall preserve thee..."

Proverbs 2:10 & 11 (KJV)

Every man needs to endorse, apply and refer other men to this humble sexual dexterity. It is particularly useful in marital affairs, where mental stress has been identified as being ready, to take its toll. In such a union, mental stress would be removed, anxiety doused and partners will sort out issues in no time. The moment her nerves are calm, the woman, a family pivot so created personally by God would take honorable steps, to safeguard the survival of the relationship she's built. She's got the capacity that's also a heavenly aptitude to do so.

Although the man was created before the woman, he taught her all she knew by his own divine wisdom, all the same, he's not superior. In fact, the woman was created to have certain higher qualities than the man. **That was why God did not create Eve at the very moment He got the rib out of Adam.** God actually spent more time, to prepare a higher quality being to perform certain roles, and hence, be an appropriate help for Adam. As such, the design of Eve must have required taking the rib God extracted from Adam to somewhere else. **That was why He had to bring Eve to Adam.**

"...And **brought** her unto the man."

Genesis 2:22 (KJV)

From Adam to Eve…

God must have used the period between the removal of the rib, and the time He **brought** *Eve back to Adam, to make the woman of His intention.* So, He made a woman having better abilities. Personal aspects where the woman exhibit better qualities might include the following…:

…Wittiness
Regardless of masculine viewpoint, most women are often wittier than an average man, particularly on social issues.

…Physical and Mental Loyalty
At all times, the woman is willing to help take up additional responsibilities whenever her man needs help.

…Loving Heart
In women, the higher capacity with which to love and care is a deliberate creation of God. As such, women often contribute more inputs than men, in romantic affairs.

…Humility
This is a major tool in the hands of women. Often, it is handy whenever they need to proffer ideas, and at any time modesty is the virtue needed to move ahead …on family growth.

…Endurance
The woman is not only willing to endure but often ready to fight back, when social-economic issues are set like a disaster, to submerge her family and relationship. More than men, they are resilient in the face of social worries.

…High Capability
A woman has divine aptitude which makes her work with a higher ability than an average man. They are ever mindful of and better at recurrent tasks in the home, handling multi-tasks, and using psychic powers to predict issues. Efficiently, they are better at using the power of communication.

…Beauty
Women are not just beautiful; they know how to complement their beauty with matching colors in cosmetics, clothes and accessories. They are ever captivating to men.

All these and perhaps a few other features attracted the man to his spouse from the beginning. Definitely, they are included in what a man loves in his wife. They are part of the qualities for which a woman is perceived as virtuous, of course, they are part of the qualities of the woman in Proverbs chapter thirty-one, verses ten to thirty, in The Holy Bible. Regrettably, these are features that'll give way to the adverse influence of mental stress. In the meantime, a sexologist in the US affirms that, "Orgasm is a release mechanism for the body; it is able to discharge all kinds of tension." Certainly, the tension that could bring about mental torture on the woman, so much as to badly affect those distinctive features of a virtuous woman, will be contained within this pack. Then, a link between orgasm and a stress-free life is evident here.

Thank goodness, we might say at this moment. As the woman works tirelessly, the man has an antidote he could use relentlessly to reinvigorate her. By offering orgasms on a regular basis, the man could ensure that the woman too benefits maximally from sexual intercourse, in the same way he is doing. This is one of the ways, if not the most significant one, by which a man could live just fine with his wife. Indeed, with an all-embracing overview, the man craves success in his marriage and therefore, a prosperous family. The woman likewise, though in a **stepwise approach,** is praying for the same thing. Worthy of note here is that this feminine method is instructive; it has the capability to split issues into pin-point fineness before applying skills for a perfect resolution. For the fact that he's working towards the same goal as his wife, then, the man should co-opt his able companion. Cheerfully, he should *relate with her, definitely not as a weak being,* (and please take note of this) *but... "As unto a weaker vessel...."*

> "Likewise, ye husbands, dwell with them... as unto the weaker vessel...; that your prayers be not hindered."
>
> 1st Peter 3:7 (KJV)

The Bible did not refer to the woman as a weak vessel as most people tend to interpret this verse. A humble meaning for the seventh verse of first Peter chapter three is that *the woman should be treated* **as if** *(as unto)* **she is weaker than the man.** In this verse, the Bible is simply **teaching the man to pamper his spouse.** This is a lesson that is being taught as a masculine marital input. So, pampering the woman is a marital input ...that **shouldn't only precede sexual activities; rather, it should be a regular habit from the man.** This masculine input would keep the woman lively and willing to offer sexual excitement for the man.

From Adam to Eve…

It is common knowledge that every woman wants to date a man that is witty. However, it is erroneous to think that she's looking for a genius in Mathematics. A man would need to access advice on various marital issues, with support from a *help meet*. He'd need to be someone who could use the divine calling of a man to bring the best out of feminine ingenuity. This is why the man is the *head and, in a way,* this is how the man would get *placed at the helm of all affairs in his family.* Obviously, this is what a woman would want to know about… while dating. She wants to be sure she's hanging about with the right man before tying the nuptial knot. Subtly, the woman is looking for a man that could be wise enough to always apply the sense in the saying that, "Two heads are better than one." For a better insight, the Bible further clarifies that, "…Foolish [is a] king who no longer knew how to take advice." (Ecclesiastes 4:13 English Standard Version, 2011)

In all simplicity, a woman uses skills not taught within school walls, to do necessary assessment. She is able to do so due to the fact that on one hand, the **help meet aptitude** is divinely fused into her body physiology. On the other, it appears she has a special link to God via a control switch that is always turned **on**… by default. If not, on what other basis could anyone explain women's conformity with the directives in the sixteenth verse of Genesis chapter three? Clearly, this Bible verse buttresses the fact that the woman is an appropriate help for the man; **he is the one she'll always support.** So, the woman is displaying the fact that no one will ever go into a *business* endeavor with a non-beneficial partner.

According to our highly regarded American bestselling author, Naura Hayden, "When it comes to making vows, sex is very persuasive…." Now, in this book is a method by which a woman could obtain immense benefit from sex. She'll be lured out of sexual apathy, and be deeply involved in sexual activities with her spouse. Without doubt, this would create sexual excitement for the man, in the way he wanted it. Undoubtedly, where a man gets utmost sexual excitement, there he'd often want to be and, this is also true for women. Then, as soon as anyone becomes perfect with this sexual technique, there'd be the need to apply caution. The use of this sexual technique should be restricted within one's marriage, to prevent anyone from *starting a race on a track that leads to nowhere.*

"Drink waters out of thine own cistern, and running waters out of thine own well. …rejoice always with the wife of thy youth. …and be thou ravished always with her love."

Proverbs 5:15 – 19 (KJV).

Entirely, chapter five of the Book of Proverbs is *a marriage seminar for men.* According to English Standard Version, 2011, the chapter is titled, "Warning against Adultery." However, within King James' Version, the chapter is titled, "Solomon Exhorts to Wisdom," with further division into three subtitles. Proverbs chapter five, verses fifteen to nineteen is contained in the second subtitle… "He Exhorts to Contentedness, Liberality, and Chastity." The author of this book being a non-native speaker of the English language might spend ages to clarify the entire chapter. It will suffice to say that the wisdom in each word is noteworthy; for men, there is a covert search for marital success… all the way.

To enjoy marital success with zero effort, it is now clear that the man will have to utilize a humble personality to lead his woman into marital excitement. The man should involve his woman on every initiative. He should be fully aware that the woman has an almost flawless ability she could use to advance his effort, on every side of a marriage. Hence, it's got to be, from Adam to Eve; clearly, this is God's pathway to a successful marriage, regardless of whatever the issue is, sexual or other.

Exposed here in this book, is the sexual prowess that is sought after by every man, well-known to everyone, and is yet untapped by no one. Without a doubt, it is a better alternative to cunnilingus, not just owing to its efficiency, but for its social acceptability as well. The few people using it do not deploy it extensively. They often use it for much less than thirty seconds, a time far too short for the woman to build-up an appreciable sexual excitement from it. It is certain that many are unaware of its potential, particularly when the application is prolonged and at a position convenient to both partners.

While both the man and the woman in a marriage are in favor of social-financial elevation for their family, the woman, more frequently, has a greater consideration for prudence and a humble beginning. Little wonder there's an aspect in every culture that unambiguously points to the woman as the family pivot. Therefore, it is important to ensure that she's given an abundant opportunity to perform her natural role. Apparently, every man is aware of this but conspicuously, there's one more missing link.

If the effect of a single orgasm for the man, is the same as the effect of multiple orgasms in the woman and… she has the ability to cope. If we could agree that the benefit obtainable by the man in an orgasm will copiously tally with that by the woman, when she's made to accomplish multiple orgasms. Then, it is proper for her to have it as often as she desires. Accordingly, here's where the secret of a happy marital life is rooted; it is where the woman would be dedicated to protect the success of her husband and her marriage. This is when the man (whose orgasmic occurrence is as regular as the clock) would have ensured that his wife is reinvigorated sufficiently and recurrently, to execute and excel in her God given role. If the man will fine-tune his gaze a little further, clearly, what will show up as missing is a link between feminine orgasm… and marital success. Up to the end… the man can now smile, while he places a broader smile on the lips of his spouse.

(To see a video-like representation of the image, click on the figure).
Video clip is available in eBook format only.

About the Author

Wale Joseph is a Small-Scale Business Growth Strategist. For over 20 years, he's been applying a method that could lure the woman out of sexual passivity… and in no time, prompt sexual delight for the couple. He has detailed a technique that conforms to research results that, "Women's (and by extension) Couple's sexual delight could lower the incidence of sexual unfaithfulness in both men and women" …to save marriages.

He is the author of two books that could transform into essential tools in every marriage.

He's married with grown up kids.

Contact: familypivot@gmail.com

Or +234 1 802 101 6239 (SMS Only)

Readers' comment is a treasure…
Kindly make use of…

https://www.familypivot.com/comment

This eBook is also available in other formats…

1. Print… on Amazon.
   Link: https://www.amazon.com/dp/9789417152

2. FATE: eBook
   a. PDF
   b. Audio Format in PDF.
   c. Précis volume for VIPs in PDF.
   d. Executable Format.
   • Link: https://www.familypivot.com/shop/

Requirement for the eBook in Executable Format.
a. The eBook will open only on a PC.
b. Operating System: Microsoft Windows.

c. Length: 35,000 words approximately.
d. Features:
- Audio… five hours maximum.
- Visible eBook icon… on the desktop.
- Double click on the icon to open the eBook.
- To go beyond ***"Introduction…"*** you'll need a License Key.

For more help on the executable format, see any of the five links below.

1. From Adam to Eve… eBook's Icon on your Desktop
    https://youtu.be/Ja7sh4A621E

2. From Adam to Eve… Introduction
    https://youtu.be/An7vJ_IBRNQ

3. Structure of the eBook…
    https://youtu.be/Kq2QUupo_F0

4. Windows protected your PC…
    https://youtu.be/bU7W4fOJPsY

5. How to Unlock the eBook…
    https://youtu.be/AlVAmL29Q8Y

Of all the good things in life, only very few are impera-
tives...!
For more information, go to...
https://trevo.life/BraveSupport/home

Essentials are:
• Physical Health • Financial Health
• Emotional Health • Spiritual Health

Referral Name: Joseph Akinwunmi Adewale

Referral ID: 4654415

Trévo

Referral Name: Joseph Akinwunmi Adewale

Referral ID: 4654415

For more information, go to the link below…
https://trevo.life/BraveSupport/home

"…Glory to God in the highest, and on Earth peace, good will toward men."

Luke 2:14(KJV)

9 789789 417155